"*Deepening Faith* is a comprehensive, practical, and user-friendly handbook for transforming a parish into a learning community. It includes everything from adult faith formation theory to innovative options. The parish-tested and well-researched advice and the challenging reflection questions are invaluable for parish adult faith formation leaders. Effective parish adult faith formation planning requires this handbook along with *Our Hearts Were Burning Within Us*."

— Thomas D. Sauline, DMin, Diocesan consultant for religious education

"Sr. Janet challenges us to be more proactive about building a healthy culture of life-long learning. Seasoned by experience and dialogue with adult educators around the country and the world, she guides us through the research, resources, and best practices that grow more healthy learning communities. Whether you are new to the task or have been doing this for some time, read this book! Read it together as a staff and your parish will be enriched by the treasures you find."

— Dr. Harry J. Dudley
Veteran catechist and diocesan director of religious education
Editor of *Forming Disciples for the New Evangelization*, the religion
curriculum of the Archdiocese of Washington

"Sr. Janet makes the ongoing journey of adult faith formation come alive for those just beginning and those already in the field forming disciples. What I found most helpful were the Reflection/Conversation Starters as they invited me into the book, as well as to realize I could do this in my community a step at a time."

— Mary Ann Ronan
Longtime parish faith formation director

Deepening Faith

Adult Faith Formation in the Parish

Janet Schaeffler, OP

LITURGICAL PRESS

Collegeville, Minnesota

www.litpress.org

1	2	3	4	5	6	7	8	9

Library of Congress Cataloging-in-Publication Data

Names: Schaeffler, Janet, author.
Title: Deepening faith : adult faith formation in the parish / Janet
    Schaeffler, OP.
Description: Collegeville, Minnesota : Liturgical Press, 2016.
Identifiers: LCCN 2016007164 (print) | LCCN 2016016873 (ebook) | ISBN
    9780814646526 (pbk.) | ISBN 9780814646762 (ebook)
Subjects: LCSH: Catholic Church—Adult education. | Faith development.
Classification: LCC BX921 .S33 2016 (print) | LCC BX921 (ebook) | DDC
    268/.434—dc23
LC record available at https://lccn.loc.gov/2016007164

Adult faith formation is the tool we have
to help us bring faith and life together;
to answer the questions,
to make sense of what sometimes gets all mixed up.

Then as disciples,
as evangelizers,
we answer the call to bring that Gospel to the world
so that faith and life can come together
                    for each of us and
                                for the world we touch.

Contents

Introduction

In a time of drastic change, it is the learners who inherit the future. The learned usually find themselves equipped to live in a world that no longer exists.

—Eric Hoffer, Reflections on the Human Condition

To learn and never be filled, is wisdom; to teach and never be weary, is love.

—Unknown

Awakened and energized by the Spirit, let us strengthen our commitment and intensify our efforts to help the adults in our communities be touched and transformed by the life-giving message of Jesus, to explore its meaning, experience its power, and live in its light as faithful adult disciples today. Let us do our part with creativity and vigor, our hearts aflame with love to empower adults to know and live the message of Jesus. This is the Lord's work. In the power of the Spirit it will not fail but will bear lasting fruit for the life of the world.

—US bishops, Our Hearts Were Burning Within Us, 183

Adult faith formation, the center of the church's educational mission, is a gift, a necessity, a challenge, and an inspiration for every adult today. For those of us involved in the ministry of adult faith formation, we are called to be continual learners, advocates, collaborators, and witnesses. In order to grow and deepen in this ministry, we need continually to learn fresh ways of thinking and acting.

Fortunately, we have a treasure trove of resources about adult faith formation—from our universal and local church, from researchers, and from people involved in the day-to-day ministry of adult faith formation. This book is one small addition, a support on the journey as we seek to continue to understand, appreciate, and deepen, in ourselves and others, the ways, whys, and hows of adult faith formation within our parishes and (arch)dioceses today.

There are many ways this book can be used—and reused:

- Give a copy to each member of your adult faith formation committee (or education commission, parish pastoral council, parish staff).
- Before coming to each monthly meeting, invite everyone to read one of the chapters. Beginning with chapter 1 and proceeding throughout the book might be the best way, or first choose the chapters that are most pertinent for your parish at the time.
- Begin each monthly meeting with prayer:

    As we continue our ministry, our continuing work together, we turn to you, gracious God, for it is your work that we do, the work of your Gospel.

    Let us never lose sight of our purpose and rely on our own efforts. But keep your vision before our eyes. Bring to our ministry a living sense that you, Lord, are the ground and the goal, the inspiration and the reason for all that we do.

    In this awareness, may we do today's work—our study, our reflection, our conversation—faithfully.

    In this awareness, may we do our work—our explorations, our deliberations, our listening to each other—compassionately.

    May we pause patiently to listen for your wisdom, to see with your eyes.

    May the way in which we carry out our work here this day spill over to all we do and to all to whom we minister, bringing your Good News of healing, peace, and unconditional love. Amen.

- For the first twenty minutes of the meeting, for your own growth and formation, take time for discussion on what you have previously read. The "Reflection/Conversation Starters" at the end of each chapter can be a guide as you apply the ideas and suggestions of the chapter to your unique parish community.
- There is always more to explore! The "Hands-On Helps" at the end of each chapter provide some suggestions for continued learning that can be explored by members on their own or at a subsequent meeting.

The book's layout of ten chapters can take you through one year of meetings. When a new year begins, there might be new members joining your committee (or staff). You might want to begin again. Because of new members, because of the experiences of the past year, because of the adult faith formation opportunities recently offered, because of changing needs within the people and the parish, the conversations will always be new, with growing and deepening understandings, plans, and dreams.

Blessings on the journey ahead, an extraordinary one because of God's Spirit working with you, an amazing one because of the gifts and faithfulness of each unique person working together.

1

What Is Adult Faith Formation?

Responding to Today's Searching

Now that very day two of them were going to a village seven miles from Jerusalem called Emmaus, and they were conversing about all the things that had occurred. And it happened that while they were conversing and debating, Jesus himself drew near and walked with them . . . Then they said to each other, "Were not our hearts burning [within us] while he spoke to us on the way and opened the scriptures to us?"

—Luke 24:13-15, 32

These words of the Gospel continue to ring out today in our parishes; Catholics are calling on the church to quench their thirst for a deepening of their lived faith. They realize that the catechesis they received as children simply isn't enough to continue growing in the faith as adults within today's church and world; they desire a deepened faith.

Since the Second Vatican Council, the church has sought to significantly change the role of the laity from spectators to participants, our commissioned role by baptism. The church is calling upon us to fully live our baptismal calling through participation, committed discipleship, and a deeper knowledge of the faith. Adult faith formation is the root of this participation for all the laity.

Since the close of Vatican II, the church has officially published no fewer than eight major documents calling for adults to be at the center of the church's educational mission. In their 1972 document, *To Teach as Jesus Did*, the United States bishops confirmed that adult catechesis is "situated not at the periphery of the Church's educational mission but at its center" (43). The *General Directory for Catechesis*, issued by the Vatican in 1997, also affirms that catechesis for adults "must be considered the chief form of catechesis"

(59). In the same way, our second *National Directory for Catechesis* (2005) continues the strong imperative for the centrality of adult faith formation: "The catechetical formation of adults is essential for the Church to carry out the commission given the apostles by Christ" (48A).

1999 brought the landmark document for the US church. The United States bishops published *Our Hearts Were Burning Within Us: A Pastoral Plan for Adult Faith Formation in the United States*. Along with its *Leader's Guide*, this indispensable resource is a vision as well as a strategy for adult faith formation in our parishes and (arch)dioceses. It emphasizes that, through adult faith formation, the baptized consciously grow in the life of Christ through prayer and study, reflection and experience.

What Is Adult Faith Formation?

Even though one definition that might come to mind is "intentional learning experiences that deepen, expand, and make explicit the learning in faith that is, hopefully, already part of the life of the believing community," adult faith formation goes well beyond that!

Adult faith formation is much more than programs, much more than intentionally planned learning experiences. Even the intentionally planned learning experiences can (should) happen in a myriad of ways; it is also obvious there are other ways that people learn, other ways that faith grows and deepens.

Adult learning is happening all the time: through the media, casual conversations, traveling, etc. Much learning happens in everyday life moments (starting a family, retirement, etc.) or in crisis events (illness, unemployment, etc.). Adult faith formation is happening continually throughout the totality of parish life, such as celebrating weekly liturgy, participating in parish outreach and service activities, joining with others to sign a petition for a justice issue, celebrating the sacramental life of our church, helping build a house with Habitat for Humanity, partaking in prayer groups, and seeking spiritual direction available at the parish.

Adult faith formation is much more than programs: the parish is the curriculum. Community, worship, teaching, proclamation, and outreach are unquestionably formational in our lives as Catholics. Practitioners have been reminding us for years that the entire reality of parish life is the curriculum of adult faith formation. This principle is now boldly proclaimed in the *General Directory for Catechesis*, and also *Our Hearts Were Burning Within Us*: "While the parish may *have* an adult faith formation program, it is no less true that the parish *is* an adult faith formation program" (121). "The Parish

Is the Curriculum . . . the success of such efforts (intentional efforts) rests very much on . . . 'the quality of the liturgies, the extent of shared decision making, the priorities in the parish budget, the degree of commitment to social justice'" (118).

Religious educator Maria Harris reminded us in *Fashion Me a People: Curriculum in the Church*, "The curriculum must take into account three forms: the explicit curriculum, the implicit curriculum, and the null curriculum."[1] The explicit curriculum, of course, consists of those adult faith formation offerings that are available in and through the parish: a Scripture study on the resurrection accounts, centering prayer, support groups for various life events, a series exploring the liturgy, and so forth. The implicit or hidden curriculum includes those attitudes or patterns that are part of us, that we might not even be aware of: who is included (or not included) on the parish pastoral council, how the parish budget is determined (and how much money is allocated for outreach to the needy, for instance), and even the design and setup of a room/chapel/church. The null curriculum is that which is absent. Are there thoughts, ideas, suggestions, opinions that are not being raised? Are there viewpoints and perspectives that are not being heard, that are being ignored? Are there methods, techniques for learning/human growth we might be ignoring, that we have not incorporated into our processes?

Everything we do (or do not do) teaches. Adult faith formation is not just about planning six-week programs; it is about the way a parish lives moment by moment. Adult faith formation—since it responds to the various age groups, different learning styles, people with diverse daily schedules—needs to have many forms and methods, but even before that, the entire life of the parish—everything that happens—is educating, is forming people in faith.

Adult faith formation is much more than programs; it can (and does) happen anywhere. Most adults live their faith at church 3 percent of their time; the rest of their time they are living it at home, in their neighborhoods, in their workplaces, etc. They live it and deepen it in activities such as these:

> answering a question from a coworker about what they believe
> making Lenten resolutions
> praying with their spouse/family
> struggling with a decision and talking it over with other people of faith
> forgiving at home, forgiving in their neighborhood, forgiving in their community
> responding with care, compassion, and kindness—often on the spur of the moment

Frequently, busy lives today won't allow the time for people to show up for "six-week programs" at the parish. What new models can we develop to infuse adult faith formation into everyday lives at home, in the neighborhood, at work—in the everyday spaces and places of people's lives?

Adult faith formation is much more than programs; learning to be a disciple happens during the living of life. As crucial as it is to have designed, scheduled opportunities for ongoing faith formation in parishes/regions, consider your own life; think about your family's life. When were the life-changing moments? Probably most of them happened outside of "preplanned" workshops or courses. Upon reflection, most people realize that usually their life-changing moments, their deepest faith growth, occurred during the unpredictable situations—and even crises—of normal, everyday life. Growth in faith happens in myriads of ways, especially in the living of life.

This reality underlies adult faith formation ministry, especially if we take seriously Marshall McLuhan's overwhelming reminder that "the medium is the message." Business consultant M. Rex Miller, in *The Millennium Matrix: Reclaiming the Past, Reframing the Future of the Church,* says, "Discipleship is not a small group or classroom topic. It is a lab project, a choreographed dance, an art taught under the eye of a master. It is apprehended first through demonstration, not intellectually."[2]

The Goals for Adult Faith Formation

Why do we do it? Why have church documents put so much emphasis on adult faith formation? The goals could be described in various ways; *Our Hearts Were Burning Within Us* synthesizes them into three categories, reminding us that formation is much more than knowledge:

First, "Ongoing Conversion to Jesus in Holiness of Life" (68–69). The Christian vocation is about ongoing change, transformation, and conversion. God has called us to be holy, to be our best selves; that requires constant change. This is a challenge; usually we resist change. It's been said that the only person who likes change is a wet baby. Adult faith formation—in all its forms—is one of the key ways we have to deepen this ongoing conversion, to deepen our relationship with Jesus.

Second, "Active Membership in the Christian Community" (70–71). A unique reality about the Christian faith is that we are not called by God as individuals. We don't go to God alone; we go to God as a community or we don't go. Our faith is not just a God-and-me religion. Thus, this second goal of all adult faith formation helps us continually understand and experience this, enabling everyone to accept co-responsibility for the community's mission and internal life.

Third, *"Prepare Adults to Act as Disciples in Mission to the World"* (72–73). In many ways the first two goals prepare us for this: to renew and transform the face of the earth. The role of the church/parish is to gather and to send. We live this in Eucharist; we live this in the entire life of the parish. We gather (in worship, community, formation) in order to be sent to the world.

Does this third goal scare us because it seems "too big"? We need to think of being missioned to the world as doable. Some people might ask, what can one person ever do? Some people have all they can do to care for their elderly parent(s) and advocate for their rights. Is this not responding to human need, the human need where our life experience currently reveals God's presence? Some people who are homebound might feel they can't be involved in touching the world beyond their home. My mom was very involved in a telephone ministry of calling people weekly, people she did not know (at the beginning), but whose names were given to her so she might check in with them once a week. Letter-writing about important issues of concern is another valuable way to be involved in making a difference in the issues of today.

These three goals are achieved through information and formation for the sake of transformation. First, the lives of the baptized are transformed, growing more and more into the people God created them to be. Through this personal transformation, they are then witnesses of Christ, making a difference in the world. The overarching goal of adult faith formation is a sense of mission rather than just the enhancing of membership.

Reflection/Conversation Starters

- Do the goals, schedules, budget, Sunday bulletin, website, etc., of our parish reflect the church documents that say that adult faith formation is at the center of the church's educational mission? If not, where do we start?

- If someone reviewed the opportunities for adult faith formation in our parish, what might he or she see as the reason/goal for adult faith formation?

- As an adult faith formation committee, education commission, parish pastoral council, are we aware of some of the implicit curriculum that is operative in our parish?

What might it be teaching?

Do we want this to continue or would we like to change it?

What are the steps/methods needed to change it?

   📖 Are we aware of some of the null curriculum that is operative in our parish?

What might it be teaching?

Do we want this to continue or would we like to change it?

What are the steps/methods needed to change it?

Hands-On Helps

📖 US Catholic bishops, *Our Hearts Were Burning Within Us: A Pastoral Plan for Adult Faith Formation in the United States* (along with its *Leader's Guide*) (Washington, DC: USCCB, 1999).

📖 To explore some of the consequences of not providing adult faith formation within our parishes, see Janet Schaeffler, "Adult Formation: Counting the Consequences," http://www.janetschaeffler.com/Adult_Formation_Counting _the_Consequences.pdf.

Notes

[1] Maria Harris, *Fashion Me a People: Curriculum in the Church* (Louisville, KY: Westminster John Knox, 1989), 68.

[2] M. Rex Miller, *The Millennium Matrix: Reclaiming the Past, Reframing the Future of the Church* (New York: Wiley, 2004).

2

None of Us Is as Smart as All of Us
The Who of Adult Faith Formation

A dult faith formation belongs to everyone; it permeates the parish and is the responsibility of everyone. The US bishops' pastoral letter *Our Hearts Were Burning Within Us* says that "the whole parish is responsible for catechetical ministry" (126). It goes on to delineate the four key roles for adult faith formation in a parish, but first, it strongly reminds us that adult faith formation is a ministry that belongs to all baptized adults. By the nature of baptism, each of us is called to nurture his or her faith growth. The purpose of adult faith formation is to nourish and strengthen this lifelong process, which requires learning, effort, and direction. Thus, adult faith formation is a deliberate and intentional activity of the parish community—and everyone in the parish.

The only way adult faith formation will become the lifeblood of the community is if it's owned by everyone. It is the work *of* everyone in the parish *for* everyone in the parish. We are a learning community together. The following are three of the many ways we might do this:

First, frequently—through homilies, bulletin and website notices, etc.— nudge people into reflecting on the methods they use/could use to deepen their faith. Point out the many things they are already doing but they might not see as adult formation (because it's not attending a four-week course). Continually plan opportunities—through all kinds of methods (e.g., retreats, workshops, online opportunities, resources for individual study)—that meet the various life/faith needs of the parishioners. Alert people to the many opportunities and possibilities in surrounding parishes, retreat centers, libraries, community programs, on the web, etc.

Second, continually invite the vision, suggestions, needs assessment, help, and involvement of other leadership groups and organizations within the parish with the adult faith formation committee and the education commission. Especially at times when there will be a significant parish event (parish mission or retreat, Lenten opportunity, a series at the time of a national election, a service opportunity followed by small-group reflection, etc.), invite other parish leadership groups to be intimately involved, for instance: ministers of care, liturgy commission, ministers of hospitality and environment, Christian service commission/justice and peace committee, social commission, family life committee, Knights of Columbus. Ask them what they can/will contribute, what part they can play in planning and hosting this parish opportunity.

Third (as parish staff and adult faith formation directors), never begin anything that can't continue without us. But begin lots of things! Simply encourage and empower those who are interested in this topic, this program, this opportunity to develop the skills, knowledge, and experience to keep it going—without us. People are sitting in our pews with many gifts, waiting to be encouraged, to continually be formed and deepened in their faith, and are eager to share, to be called forth to live their baptismal commitment. The ministry of adult faith formation belongs to all of us.

Adult Faith Formation Director

Even though it is true that adult faith formation is the work of everyone, whenever it's said that everyone is *in charge*, the reality is that no one is. *Our Hearts Were Burning Within Us* acknowledges this: "Each parish will designate an adult faith formation leader—authorized by the pastor and personally involved in ongoing formation—to assume primary responsibility for implementing the ministry of adult faith formation" (135).

This person's role is comprehensive and all-encompassing. It is not simply a planner of programs, but a unifier, an encourager. Flowing from the title of *Our Hearts Were Burning Within Us*, the role of the adult faith formation director can be said to be "the keeper of the flame"—keeping before everyone the necessity and joy—of faith formation as a lifelong journey and the reality that everything a parish does is forming our lives in faith.

Committees/Teams for Adult Faith Formation Ministry

Adult faith formation ministry is not a ministry of one person! Even though one staff person or one generous "volunteer" may be asked and prepared to coordinate it, it is a ministry of the many. In addition to naming the reality that all in leadership are responsible, *Our Hearts Were Burning Within Us* calls each parish to have an adult faith formation team (or committee) that is "committed to and responsible for implementing the parish vision and plan for adult faith formation" (142). "The parish has a functioning adult faith formation team that is formally recognized in the parish leadership structure" (144).

Systems scientist Peter Senge in *The Fifth Discipline* talks about two kinds of visions: A sowed vision is developed by only one person. One person's vision is foisted on others. People are not invested. When there's any difficulty, they will abandon the vision. A shared vision is collaborative. People work together to name the vision; hence, they are committed. They will fight to the death to accomplish the vision. Adult faith formation will be very different in our parishes when it is envisioned, planned, and implemented by a shared vision, by a dedicated group that is representative of and responsible to their co-journeyers in the faith within their parish.

What are some of the roles and tasks of the adult faith formation committee? The first and underlying role is their own ongoing formation and growth in faith. All adults, of course, are called to continual learning and deepened commitment. As a parish leader, there's almost an added responsibility. If our area of parish leadership is adult faith formation, how can we not want to—and be excited to—continue to grow in faith? Fortunately today there are so many ways to continue learning and growing in faith: homilies, the various programs and small groups already offered in parishes, numerous Catholic periodicals and books, retreats, online learning opportunities—to name just a few. To be active in our own formation is our first role. We model for others what we're calling them to do.

Another role of an adult faith formation committee is to network with organizations and committees within the parish and the diocese. We never work alone. The committee/team works closely with the parish's adult faith formation coordinator or parish catechetical leader. Everyone ministers with the pastor, who has responsibility for the ongoing faith development of the parish community. (Our network doesn't stop at the parish. There is also the geographical region—deaneries, vicariates, etc.—and the various offices and committees of the [arch]diocese.) Networking means more than just contacting the various parish committees. As an adult faith formation committee, we invite all parish groups and organizations to work with us to create an environment that welcomes, supports, and promotes adult faith formation for all ages and in various formats.

Because we have invited other parish groups and organizations to work with us in this important ministry, we need to visit with these groups or their leaders and let them know the vision and plans of the adult faith formation team/committee. When we meet with them, we express that we are eager to listen to their concerns and interests regarding their own faith growth, listen to how they perceive the needs of the parish, and then attempt to plan programs that are a response to their interests and needs.

Our parishes and (arch)dioceses are composed of a diversity of cultural and ethnic groups. As we listen to these various groups, as well as the parish leadership groups, and then plan for their needs, this creates multiple opportunities. Diversity—within all parishioners, because of the various leadership groups—offers the community many gifts. We are richer because of each other. Having met and listened to the various groups within the parish and having become more and more aware of the gifts our parish has because of its diversity, those we met with may be able to assist the committee or team in gathering information for a program, providing assistance with a program (especially one they suggested), and helping with promotion and publicity.

Some of the many other tasks of an adult faith formation committee include the following (some of which we'll look at more closely in subsequent chapters):

- ✓ Visioning realistically and imaginatively for the future
- ✓ Deepening an understanding of the principles of adult learning
- ✓ Carrying out continual needs assessment
- ✓ Researching resources
- ✓ Assisting in formulating the budget
- ✓ Designing/planning/scheduling programs and processes for adult faith formation
- ✓ Providing marketing and promotion
- ✓ Setting a hospitable environment for adult formation
- ✓ Infusing adult formation into existing parish programs/structures
- ✓ Organizing ongoing evaluation

Within all these tasks, especially the design of programs and resources, two (of many) guidelines are important. First, in the design of formation opportunities, include offerings from all six dimensions of Catholic life. *Our Hearts Were Burning Within Us* (88–96) provides a guideline: "Knowledge of the

Faith" (doctrine, teaching, Scripture); "Liturgical Life" (worship, sacraments); "Moral Formation" (morality, justice, lifestyle); "Prayer" (devotion, contemplation, retreats); "Communal Life" (strengthening relationships); "Missionary Spirit" (living and spreading the Good News).

Second, in addition to offering specific and intentional programs on Catholic social teaching, all programming should be infused with justice and peace themes, for this touches all that we are as Catholic Christians. Our adult formation efforts are centered in the Gospel; Jesus, as the center of our life and discipleship, always calls us to living and acting in justice and peace.

Subcommittees for Adult Faith Formation Ministry

The more the merrier! *Our Hearts Were Burning Within Us* calls each parish to have an adult faith formation team (or committee); the joy (and challenge) is that adult faith formation within a parish doesn't have to be completely done by this one committee or team. There are many ways to reach out to and involve others, especially with the formation of subcommittees.

For instance, one of the important steps in the implementation of the parish's adult faith formation plan is marketing and publicity. For this one purpose a subcommittee can be created of parishioners who have interest and/or specific expertise—such as the following:

IT experts
marketing specialists
employees in advertising offices
journalists and/or English teachers, photographers
TV or radio station personalities/managers/ employees
employees of companies that create signage
webmasters

bloggers
YouTube visionaries or videographers
graphic arts experts
sound/recording experts
press experts
communications professionals
publicists
advertising executives

Catechists of Adults: How Many? Why?

How many catechists does your parish have for children and youth? Twenty? Thirty-five? Fifty? Seventy-five or more? How much time, planning, and resources go into the formation and care of these catechists? Rightly so!

How many catechists does your parish have for the adults within your parish? How many adults are within your parish? How many varied needs surface from these adults? How many diverse opportunities can be provided and offered for ongoing growth and formation?

Our Hearts Were Burning Within Us reminds us, "Each parish will have access to trained catechists to serve the diverse adult faith formation efforts of the parish or region" (149). "Parishes provide recognition for their catechists of adults and funding assistance for their formation" (153).

A friend of mine continually tells the story (to anyone who will listen) that years ago she came to me about beginning a Scripture study group in the parish. I replied that I'd be glad to do it—with her. Mary already had a good foundation in Scripture; she wanted to—and did—continue her own study/formation. After a year, I invited her to continue as leader of the group. That was not her original intent, but she continues to do it today—over twenty-five years later.

As we look at all that adult faith formation can mean in today's parish, are we providing for time, planning, and resources to train catechists of adults for the multiple needs and opportunities within a parish? Let's imagine just some possibilities:

> groups who pray the Scriptures with *lectio divina*
>
> business executives who meet for prayer and discussion about their role in the business world as Christian leaders
>
> the many small groups that come together for Scripture study and faith sharing
>
> the various peer groups that meet for everyday life needs (cancer support, grief support, caregivers, mothers of young children, married couples, seeking employment, etc.)
>
> those who participate in online book clubs and/or faith sharing groups
>
> parishioners preparing for marriage or baptism
>
> parishioners having a process or place to reflect upon the various service/ outreach opportunities in which they participate
>
> RCIA catechists, for all the periods, in various formats

Reflection/Conversation Starters

Ministering with Others

> 📖 Which of our adult faith formation opportunities can be coplanned and cohosted by multiple parish leadership groups?
>
>> Which groups would we invite to collaborate?
>>
>> What difference might that make in the offering? for parishioners?

📖 Are each of our adult faith formation opportunities able to continue without me/us?

📖 Who is waiting to be encouraged to use their gifts?

📖 Does the adult faith formation director encourage all leadership groups/ organizations within the parish to reflect on how all of parish life is forming people: In everything that we are living and doing, and in ways we are functioning as a parish (our programs, our guidelines and procedures, our ministries and outreach), what are we teaching people about God, about faith and life, about prayer, about being church, about justice and peace, about living and bringing about the reign of God?

Adult Faith Formation Committee

📖 Who in our parish could/will we invite to be part of our parish's adult faith formation team/committee? How will we ensure that this committee is representative of the parish—its ages, its cultures, its various theological viewpoints, its spiritualities, its stages in life?

📖 How will we provide for new members to join and be incorporated within the committee?

📖 What will we do to support this committee to

continually deepen their own faith,

grow as a community together,

learn and understand the meaning of adult faith formation in today's church,

appreciate how adults learn,

explore the various methods of adult learning and formation,

survey the resources available for adult faith formation?

Subcommittees

📖 For what areas of adult faith formation ministry might we create subcommittees? Hospitality? Environment? Technology? Resource center?

📖 How will we reach out and help people discern their gifts for membership on these subcommittees, so they are serving from their strengths, rather than just filling holes?

Catechists for Adults

📖 How many catechists for adults does our parish need right now? How many will it need within the coming year(s)?

📖 What would be the best way to recruit parishioners to be catechists for adults?

📖 What kind of formation would these catechists need? What is already available for them?

Hands-On Helps

📚 Donal Dorr, *Faith at Work: A Spirituality of Leadership* (Collegeville, MN: Liturgical Press, 2007).

📚 For two examples of parish-wide programs that involved many parishioners in the planning, see Janet Schaeffler, "Moving into the Future through a Parish Synod," http://www.janetschaeffler.com/Moving_into_the_Future _through_a_Parish_Synod.pdf; and "The Planning Process Involves Everyone," http://www.janetschaeffler.com/Planning_Process_involves_Everyone .pdf.

📚 *Our Hearts Were Burning Within Us*, 142–48, spells out many of the roles of the adult faith formation committee/team. Several of these, of course, happen within meetings, or are begun at meetings. Meetings are the stuff of parish life!

In reality, it's more than that. In his syndicated column of January 26, 2003, Fr. Ron Rolheiser reminds us that "Pentecost happened at a meeting! . . . Meetings are the 'Upper room,' . . . we are waiting there, with others, for God to do something in us and through us that we can't do all by ourselves, namely, create community with each other and bring justice, love, peace, and joy to our world."[1]

Thus, some steps for sacred and successful meetings as we plan adult faith formation for the journey:

1. Have an agenda and minutes of the meetings. Remember, "If you don't know where you are going, you might end up somewhere else." Members should receive the agenda, minutes, reports, and any items to consider at least a week before the meeting.

2. Start and end on time. Put leftover items on the next agenda. If this happens often, consider decreasing the number of items at each meeting.

3. When the meeting begins, anyone who is not present is assigned a "buddy" who will contact the missing member within forty-eight hours in order to share what happened at the meeting.

4. One archdiocese has a guideline: "Every gathering of adults, whether those gatherings be meetings or catechetical sessions, will include prayer and reflection, study, business and evaluation." Prayer and formation keep us focused on our mission. We're the church, the people of God, not a corporation. Don't skimp on the time for prayer and formation.

5. Give every member a voice and a chance to participate. When someone speaks overenthusiastically about an issue/project, watch for the "bandwagon effect." Invite other ways of creatively viewing the topic, to see it from all sides, before making a decision. Subcommittees of two or more members might want to work on particular aspects/projects.

6. The chair is a facilitator/guide. This person ensures discussion and action. His or her role is not to "do" everything.

7. Identify a "host" for each new member and any guests. Your image as a committee will be enhanced. Parishioners will want to work on this committee/team.

8. Never forget the most important issue: Where do we go from here? Who does what, by when? Don't let a meeting end without determining the next step, even if it is only an incremental one.

9. Publicize the work of the adult faith formation committee/team. Let the parish know that the vision, the programs are planned by many people from the parish.

10. Spend the last few minutes of the meeting "checking out" how the meeting went for everyone and in what ways the next meeting might be more productive. It might be a simple discussion. Members might give a word/phrase to describe their feelings about the meeting. They might complete this sentence: I'm glad we _____; I wish we had _____.

11. Continually recognize, acknowledge, and reward the work of every member.

Notes

[1] Ron Rolheiser, "Pentecost Happened at a Meeting," January 26, 2003, http://ronrolheiser.com/pentecost-happened-at-a-meeting/#.V2lwytIwiUk.

3
Laying the Foundation
Before the Programming

*A*dult faith formation opportunities and processes (an integrated and inclusive formation plan) cannot be created out of a vacuum. The reality and experience of being a learning community flows first from another reality. There are various factors, foundational underpinnings, that are crucial to the success of adult faith formation in a parish. These serve to support and provide the groundwork for adult faith formation. They can be described in answer to the question, what is a vibrant parish?

Some realities that quickly come to mind—and can be witnessed and experienced—in parishes around the world are the following:

an innate spirit of invitation, welcome, and hospitality

liturgy that is alive, reverent, inclusive, participative, and sending-forth

an awareness of the needs of others, commitment to justice, peace, and social teaching with practical action locally and globally

a spirit of collaboration that recognizes, discerns, and calls forth the unique strengths and gifts of all the faithful, laity and clergy

a call to a way of life, a commitment to discipleship, rather than only a feeling of membership

"When these various elements of parish life are weak or lacking, formal programs for adults typically do not flourish; when they are vibrant and strong, they create an over-all climate of active participation and living faith that can only benefit the parish's intentional formation efforts with adults. Thus, while the parish may *have* an adult faith formation program, it is no less true that the parish *is* an adult faith formation program" (*Our Hearts Were Burning Within Us*, 121).

Pastoral Planning for Adult Faith Formation

How do we plan for adult formation? In some parishes (not yours), one or two people think of an idea for an adult faith formation program. Eight to twelve people show up. Three months later, the same one or two people think of another idea and the same eight to twelve people come.

People wonder why it's not working.

Adult faith formation—like anything worthwhile—has to be systematically planned. It can't be sporadic; it can't belong to just a few people.

Adult faith formation, as the work of the parish, needs strategic, pastoral planning. In reality, programming is not the first thing that happens, even though that is the most visible part of adult faith formation ministry. Much needs to precede it! Programming is built upon a strong foundation or it won't work; it will soon topple. The behind-the-scenes work of building the foundation is the most important work, which will provide the support for the programs.

What Is Our Vision?

"Where there is no vision, the people will perish" (see Prov 29:18). Rooted in God's vision for us, we need to concretely name how we, as a parish, desire and will commit ourselves to living that vision in this time and place. In *Excellent Catholic Parishes* filmmaker and author Paul Wilkes reminds us, "What the vast majority of Catholic parishes lack is not priests or resources, but vision, energy and hope."[1] The following questions can help us determine our vision:

- ✓ How do we want to bring about the reign of God in our part of the world?
- ✓ What do we want to be as a parish?
- ✓ How would we like our parish described by others? What do we need to accomplish that?
- ✓ As a parish and a learning community, where are we headed?
- ✓ Do we know why we are committed to adult faith formation as a parish?
- ✓ How is adult faith formation connected to the pastoral planning of the entire parish?

When we dream our vision for adult faith formation, it is important that many people be involved in the conversation. If it's only one staff person, it will never work.

If it's only our committee or team, it's not broad enough. It can begin there, but involve others who have insights and leadership roles in the parish. Talk to parishioners, representing all ages, walks of life, cultures, with various needs, and ask them about their dreams, interests, and needs.

The vision always needs to be revisited. The parish will change, times change, the needs of the people change. There are various ways to continually reassess the vision, needs, successes, and challenges; periodically answering these questions might bring new insights:

✓ Who are we today? Who do we want to be?

✓ What are the factors that have been critical to our successes?

✓ What are our strengths as a parish?

✓ What have been some of our successful adult faith growth offerings in the past five years in our parish? What do we use to determine our success?

✓ What are the challenges we have within the parish at this time as we strive to become an adult-centered learning community?

✓ What are some of the external forces over which we have no control that might impact adult learning and adult faith formation?

✓ What are the needs of the adults in our parish and how are they changing?

✓ Are there changing forces that are in competition and/or making it difficult for us to achieve our vision of adult faith formation?

✓ Is our own internal environment changing? Is that helpful or detrimental?

✓ Are there demographics of adults, specific needs/groups of adults, who are not being provided for in our parish?

✓ Are there things that need to be changed—within us, within our parish—to encourage adults to become more active in their ongoing faith growth?

Our Beliefs/Assumptions

Once we have taken time to vision who we are, where we are heading as a parish in adult faith formation, it is helpful to look at our beliefs and assumptions. What is it that we—and the parishioners—may take for granted? It might be beliefs that are "givens," which we may never have really stopped to think about. Frequently, too, if and when we do pause and think about them, we realize that they are limited. Because we have been living with them for so long, we may find that they served us well at one time, but have we now grown beyond them?

We have learned much about passing on the faith, about catechetics, about adult faith formation. As we've learned, we ask, have our beliefs and assumptions grown and changed . . . or are some of the ones we've lived with for a long time still operative? To help us reflect on this, we can also ask these questions:

- ✓ Do our actions show that we believe that all resources, spaces, scheduling on the calendar should be done first for children and youth; then whatever is left over goes to adults?
- ✓ Do parishioners—and parish leaders—believe that, because of limited resources, the parish can't afford formation programs for both children and adults?
- ✓ Do our actions show that we think of adult faith formation as a "class" or "course" at the parish that people need to attend?
- ✓ Do our actions show that ongoing continual growth in the faith stops at confirmation?
- ✓ Do people believe that adult formation is only a personal thing?
- ✓ Do people assume that they've learned all they need to know?
- ✓ Do people perceive the church and adult faith formation as irrelevant to their "real" life, with outdated ideas and judgmental attitudes?
- ✓ Do people think of adult faith formation as only for those who are retired and have a lot of time on their hands, not for busy singles or young professionals who are raising a family?

Naming and understanding the beliefs and assumptions of the staff, the parish leadership groups, and all parishioners is crucial, for these beliefs affect the attitudes, feelings, acceptance of the ways of parish life, and people's participation in the life and ministry of the parish.

In addition to naming assumptions and beliefs that might be unspoken—and have been unexamined for a while—it is also helpful to consciously decide and choose our fundamental beliefs. What do we want our undergirding assumptions to be? They will be unique for each parish; here are some possibilities:

> All adult faith formation supports people in deepening their relationship with God, connecting to others in the family of God, and fulfilling their mission to reach out in witness and service.

Faith—and adult faith formation—is meant to bring freedom, joy, and peace to our lives, not strictures and guilt.

Adult formation is planned not only to help people assume specific ministries in the parish, but to walk with them in their life transitions as well as live their faith in their everyday world. This assumption will guide the variety of topics, kinds of support groups, and resources that we strive to make available.

Adults are motivated by all-inclusive faith formation: involving them in the learning process, in practical mission, in implementing faith in action, and in building a sense of belonging and community.

There are enough resources for everyone; together—all ages—we are a learning community.

"Adults learn best when they are in conversation with other adults about things that matter" (Jane Regan in *Toward an Adult Church: A Vision of Faith Formation*).[2] This assumption/belief serves as a foundation on which to build programs that allow for adequate time for genuine conversation among the adults. Are we planning so that programs are not just lectures? Are we always looking for opportunities for conversations within our faith context—whenever adults gather? For instance, what about times such as Sunday coffee and donuts? A well-written question or series of questions on a "paper tent" placed on the tables may provide the spark for conversations about things that matter, about faith issues in real life, as well as for hospitality, inviting people to talk together.

Systems and Supports

Our parishes function in many ways. Systems and supports are in place that promote and further what we believe, where our vision is taking us. Do all of our realities of time, space, and resources support and further adult faith formation?

If adult faith formation is the core of the church's ministry, if adult faith formation is all-encompassing, nothing should happen in the parish that isn't an opportunity to educate, form, and further deepen the faith of all adults. What are some of these parish systems and supports that have the potential to promote the vision of adult faith formation? Consider the following possibilities:

✓ Are the parish bulletin and website simply announcements and news? Or are they information and formation for the purpose of transformation?

✓ What are the modes of communication that exist in our parish? With the variety that text, image, audio, and video files offer, there's practically no limit to what we can communicate with email, websites, technology, the written word, etc., as we seek to inform and form.

✓ In the areas of our parish buildings where parishioners and visitors might wait, are there magazines, articles, handouts they might read, some of which they might take home?

✓ There is wonderful service and outreach happening in and through our parishes and in people's personal lives. Do we provide time and space for reflection on it, so people have a chance to realize what happened to them, not just what they did for others, but how they were changed? What did they learn? How will their lives be different now? How did they meet Jesus?

✓ Some of the "systems and supports," too, directly involve the interactions of people. *Our Hearts Were Burning Within Us* reminds us of the way Jesus ministered: joining people in their daily concerns; walking with them on the path of life; asking them questions; listening closely as people talked about their joys, hopes, griefs, and worries. In addition to being given a warm welcome, are parishioners cared about and asked more than, "What are you doing later today?" At a parish function, do people always sit with their friends or does someone in leadership gently connect them to others who have dealt with the same griefs and anxieties, joys and dreams?

Having created a vision, named the beliefs and assumptions, and examined the systems and foundations, we are on the road of pastoral planning, of creating a two-to-four-year plan to meet the needs of our parish.

The Components of a Pastoral Plan

Having looked at many of the first (necessary and crucial) steps for pastoral planning, what are the components of an actual plan? A plan should include "goals and objectives specific to the parish community and include the regular assessment of progress toward the achievement of those goals and objectives. It should devise a schedule of catechetical activities" (*National Directory for Catechesis*, chap. 9, 60A).

Here's a summary of how to develop a possible plan:

✓ Identify your vision for adult faith formation.
✓ Identify the role of staff and recruit/form parish committee/team.
✓ Name the strengths, challenges, and current "face of the parish."

✓ Examine the parish assumptions about adult faith formation.

✓ Look at all that is going on that supports growth in faith for adults.

✓ Do a needs assessment of the adults within your parish.

✓ Prioritize what can be done.

✓ Set a timeline.

✓ Establish a two-to-four-year plan for implementation.

Therefore, these are some possible components of a parish plan for adult faith formation:

✓ Parish mission statement

✓ Parish mission statement for catechesis

✓ Parish vision statement for adult faith formation

✓ Name the leadership model

✓ Goals for adult faith formation for the following two to four years

✓ Strategies and objectives flowing from the goals

✓ Implementation process
  ◆ Budget
  ◆ Marketing/publicity
  ◆ Facilities
  ◆ Timeline
  ◆ Schedule

✓ Methods of evaluation
  ◆ Individual programs
  ◆ Annual evaluation of plan
  ◆ Evaluation from the standpoint of the staff, committee, facilitators

Some Fundamental Reminders about Parish Planning for Adult Faith Formation

First, it's never ending! The parish is always changing. Even though the plan may be "set" for two to four years, it always needs to be evaluated. Is it meeting the current needs of our parishioners?

Second, a successful plan touches everyone. How can the most people have input into it? How will we provide for people's voices, their needs, dreams, and interests, to be heard as we explore the questions: Who are we as a parish? What are we about? What has to happen if we are to continue to be disciples of Jesus in the next five years?

Third, continually use various means to do needs assessment, to hear the interests and needs of all the adults of our parish:

> What are their life issues—family, work, suffering/grief, relationships, etc.?
>
> What are the life tasks facing them in the particular age stages?
>
> What are the significant milestones/transitions being faced—moving, career changes, empty nest, retirement, illness, divorce, death of loved ones?
>
> What are the religious needs—relating Scripture to today's life, making moral decisions, living the teachings of the church, understanding the sacraments?
>
> What are the spirituality needs—growing in relationship with God, living as disciples in everyday life, deepening prayer, spiritual practices, etc.?
>
> What are the lived experiences, needs, and dreams of those from each cultural community in our parish?

Fourth, the needs, interests, and understandings of people differ! Listening to the needs of the people will probably result in various tracks within a pastoral plan for adult faith formation to allow parishioners to follow their interests and to minister out of their strengths.

Fifth, everything we do teaches. Thus, the very act of creating the plan has the potential to help parishioners deepen their realization of mission. The mission of a parish—and of each parishioner—is the mission of Christ—to reveal the good news of God's love. How concretely does your parish do that, especially in its adult faith formation processes?

Adult Faith Formation Responds to Life Needs

Throughout this look at laying the foundation for adult faith formation, we've realized that responding to life needs is crucial. Over the years, research about adult learning has demonstrated that among adults engaged in learning, 83 percent do so because of life changes and most are drawn to topics related to their current everyday needs (Robert M. Smith, *Learning How to Learn: Applied Theory for Adults*).[3] This translates, of course, to adult faith formation. Everything we do needs to link faith and everyday life together. As an example, let's explore one life change/life need and examine some possibilities:

How are we responding to the needs of today's unemployed? Many of our parishes have reached out: job fairs that match employers with people who are searching for jobs; parish website pages with speakers/helps/reflections for this difficult time; on-site speakers addressing various issues to help people deal with the reality, the implications of these economic times. Here are some other possibilities to try:

> Rather than sitting at home, people who are unemployed might appreciate a place to gather at their own parish. Create a coffeehouse atmosphere. Invite people for given hours each day to drop in for coffee, prayer, discussion, a time to just be with other people.

> This might be the ideal time to organize more volunteer projects of people helping others. Invite people who are unemployed to take a leadership role. Don't forget conversation times, giving people a chance to talk about what is happening to them during these times.

> When was the last time your adult faith formation program explored the many ways/methods of prayer? Prayer, of course, is always a part of our lives, but at crisis times people have a tendency to turn to prayer. This might provide the opportunity to explore our rich tradition of prayer and deepen people's awareness of all we have. Open the church once a day or once a week. Encourage your parishioners to take time for stillness in prayer. You might offer different forms of prayer on different days: quiet time, Liturgy of the Hours, Taizé prayer, centering prayer, *lectio divina*, etc.

> Many websites, blogs, and articles give tips for saving and cutting costs. Host a conversational swap meet. Invite people to bring their ideas of how they've simplified their lives—what's working, what's not.

> Have we ever explored the role of leisure in our programs? During unemployment, this, of course, is not leisure that has been chosen, but people find themselves in a new situation. When we live in a world that glorifies work, puts all our identity in work, we don't know how to live Sabbath and participate in leisure. Perhaps this is a time that we can all learn anew (or for the first time).

> Create support groups. Bringing people together (in face-to-face groups or through online discussion groups) to share their feelings, struggles, joys, and hopes can be supportive and faith-filled. Begin groups for those who are unemployed, the families of the unemployed, the employers who have had to let people go, etc.

> Invite people to book clubs that discuss books that touch upon today's realities and what we might do about them. Two that might be tried are *Not Working: People Talk About Losing a Job and Finding Their Way in Today's Changing Economy* by DW Gibson (New York: Penguin, 2012);

The (Un)Common Good: How the Gospel Brings Hope to a World Divided by Jim Wallis (Grand Rapids, MI: Brazos, 2014).

Reflection/Conversation Starters

📖 In an ideal world, how would we describe a vibrant parish? How would we describe the vibrancy of our parish?

📖 How might we engage various groups within our parish (the parish pastoral council, commissions, ushers, catechists, St. Vincent de Paul Society, men's club, women's club, etc.) in a conversation on what it is that makes our parish vibrant, alive, life-giving, supportive, welcoming?

📖 What is the mission statement of our parish?

📖 Can we write a vision statement for adult faith formation that flows from our parish mission statement?

📖 What are the unspoken or, more important, the unexamined, taken-for-granted beliefs about adult faith formation that are alive in our parish?

📖 What would we like the underlying assumptions and beliefs about adult faith formation to be in our parish? How might we begin to make those a reality in the awareness of our people?

📖 What is going on in our parish that supports adult faith formation, that supports an adult way of living and growing in the faith?

📖 Once we've examined and utilized all the present systems and supports, what new ones might we establish to meet the needs of our parish?

📖 What would be the advantages of having a two-to-four-year plan for adult faith formation for our parish, rather than planning programs from month to month?

📖 What would be some things to do so that pastoral planning truly is a plan for, by, and with the community, rather than only one person's agenda?

📖 Do the steps of our pastoral planning also look beyond our front door? Do we look at the needs of those in our neighborhood, our community—as well as our "registered parishioners"?

📖 Are our parishioners aware of our pastoral plan for adult faith formation?

Hands-On Helps

Approach to Needs Assessment

🌿 There are, of course, various ways to do needs assessment within your parish: evaluation of current goals and programs; studying the demographics of your area (through your parish census as well as statistics available from your city and county); paying attention to local news stories; parish surveys (written, phone calls, interviews, online, etc.); one-time think tanks or focus groups; parish assemblies; observing what is capturing the imagination and interest of adults in current books and movies; listening closely to what parishioners talk about (whenever they gather, wherever you meet them); noting what is not being talked about, etc.

Of course, needs assessment should be continual, for life situations are always changing. George Bernard Shaw said, "The only man I know who behaves sensibly is my tailor; he takes my measurements anew each time he sees me. The rest go on with their old measurements and expect me to fit them."

🌿 In all that we do to assess needs, Appreciative Inquiry can guide us in the types of questions we ask.[4] Appreciative Inquiry, a way of being and seeing, is a methodology that is positive and affirming, and moves individuals and communities forward. Here are some possible questions for parishioners—with an Appreciative Inquiry focus:

1. When you are feeling best about your membership in our parish, what part of parish life comes to mind?

2. What is the single most important thing our parish has contributed to your life?

3. What can you envision our parish doing in the next two to three years to help you and our people deepen your relationship with Christ, to living faith in everyday life?

4. When have you felt most welcomed and included at our parish? What in particular did people say or do that made you feel welcomed and included? How can our parish be more welcoming to parishioners, to inactive parishioners or visitors?

5. In your opinion, what are the two or three greatest examples of vibrancy (life) in our parish?

6. If you could imagine or change our parish in any way, what one to three things would you do to enhance its life and vitality?

❧ For a sample outline of a think tank (to do needs assessment), see Janet Schaeffler, "Ideas Mushroom in a Think Tank," http://www.janetschaeffler .com/Ideas_Mushroom_in_a_Think_Tank.pdf.

Notes

[1] Paul Wilkes, *Excellent Catholic Parishes: The Guide to Best Places and Practices* (Mahwah, NJ: Paulist Press, 2001), 151.

[2] Jane E. Regan, *Toward An Adult Church: A Vision of Faith Formation* (Chicago: Loyola Press, 2002), 162.

[3] Robert M. Smith, *Learning How to Learn: Applied Theory for Adults* (Westchester, IL: Follett, 1982).

[4] *Center for Appreciative Inquiry*, "What is Appreciative Inquiry (AI)?" http://www .centerforappreciativeinquiry.net/more-on-ai/what-is-appreciative-inquiry-ai/.

4

Continuing to Build

Before the "New" Programming

When it was published, *Our Hearts Were Burning Within Us* brought renewed enthusiasm for adult faith formation in our parishes and (arch)dioceses. Perhaps one of the "drawbacks" of this landmark document was that parish leadership began to think they hadn't been doing anything; they now needed to start from scratch.

Rather, the reality often is that much has been going on to enable and support the faith growth of the adults in our parishes. Let's explore this reality through these lenses: some things to do to get started; principles to remember as we begin; intensify what is already going on in adult faith formation; realize that everything we do is formative; infuse formation into all that is already happening.

Some Things to Do to Get Started

First, rejoice that we have *Our Hearts Were Burning Within Us* and other church documents that assert the primacy of adult faith formation. Today, parishes (and many dioceses) have worked diligently to put into place a pastoral plan for the future—looking at their strengths, needs, and challenges. In reality, though, we as a church in this nation have had in our history only one pastoral plan—that of a Catholic school system. In the early days of the immigrant church, this was important and all resources, energy, personnel, and much of the buildings went into this plan for the future of the American church. (It may need to continue; it may need to be revised; new forms of it may be needed.) But *Our Hearts Were Burning Within Us* reminds us that we are at a new time in our history; we need to read the signs of the times; we need to respond to the challenges of a new church and a new culture.

Second, study *Our Hearts Were Burning Within Us* with as many groups in your parish as possible. A convenient leader's guide accompanies the plan.

The plan is not just a visioning of the primacy of adult formation, but also suggests concrete approaches—making study (and implementation) on the parish level very possible.

Third, the pastoral plan, although it certainly acknowledges Jesus as teacher, also very graphically helps us see Jesus the listener. The implication, of course, is that this is what we are also called to. Reflect with the staff, parish pastoral council, and other parish leaders: How do we journey with people? How do we ask questions and listen as parishioners speak of their joys, hopes, griefs, and anxieties? How do we share faith? For adult formation to take root and become effective, we need to accept people where they are, hear their stories, listen attentively.

Fourth, each parish is unique; each parish will respond to the need for adult faith formation differently. Don't do something just because another parish is doing it. Don't do something because we are comparing ourselves to others.

A Few Key Principles to Remember

1. Don't let formation be seen as "religious education." Faith formation— our ongoing journey in faith—is much broader. It is about information, formation, and transformation.

2. *Our Hearts Were Burning Within Us*—and all we do today—calls for all ministers to work together, because everything we do is formative. Working together—not alone—forms us to be a community, as leaders who model collaboration in ministry. Shouldn't pastoral staff meetings, then, exhibit such mutuality? Might not staff meetings include prayer, formation, community-building, visioning, and collaborating together as one group of ministers rather than mere reporting of "this is what I'm doing in my area"?

3. Proclamation, teaching, worship, service, and community life form us. Our role as leaders is to link all these components of parish life into an interconnected journey of faith.

4. Faith formation flows primarily from our shared worship every Sunday. When we place formation of adults at the center of our catechetical ministry, it is necessarily a liturgical catechesis.

5. Adult formation calls for a model of catechesis that sees all participants as learners. The days of the "expert" and the "ignorant" cannot be continued. Human experience is the beginning point of adult catechesis.

6. Use adult learning principles whenever adults gather (e.g., sacramental preparation, parish council and commissions, etc.).

7. Adult catechesis forms people not only for membership within the church as an institution but as an evangelizing community in service and mission to the world.

Intensify What Is Already Going On in Adult Faith Formation

Much has been going on—within our parishes and (arch)dioceses—to enable and support the faith growth of today's adults. Homilies and our liturgical experiences do that; the reading materials that are provided through the parish bulletin, the many Catholic periodicals, our parish website, and the various Catholic websites do that; the sacramental programs for parents and families do that—as well as the many other intentional opportunities and offerings, and the community life of the parish.

As parishes plan for adult faith formation, then, one of the first places to begin is to look at what is already going on. Look at the various groups or categories of adults in our parish; think about the ministry and the programming that occurs on an individual, small-group, large-group, and parish-wide basis. The following are just a few of the many groups of people who might be in our parishes. Who else is there? What is happening for each group?

Parishioners in early adulthood
Parishioners in middle adulthood
Parishioners in mature adulthood
Parishioners in older adulthood

Married couples
Engaged couples
Unmarried singles

Divorced and separated
Widows and widowers

Couples with children
Single parents
Parents of infants and young children
Parents returning to church now that their children are of school age
Parents of preteens and teens
Parents whose teens are about to get their driver's license
Parents of the bride and groom

Parents experiencing the empty-nest syndrome

Parents of children with special needs
Physically handicapped adults
Adults with special needs

Grieving adults
Grieving parents
Chronically ill/dying adults
Spouses/relatives of chronically ill/dying

Military personnel/spouses
Unemployed/unemployable
Retired
Those nearing retirement
Adults who work/career persons
Parish leaders/lay ministry formation

Nonparticipating parishioners
Non-Catholic adults in the surrounding community

Adults caring for aged in their homes	Grandparents
Adults in family/personal crisis	Grandparents who are raising
Adults in transition	grandchildren
Highly mobile adults	Infirm adults
Immigrants	Adults in extended care facilities
Non-English speaking adults	Spouses/relatives of the infirm

For a more complete list of people who might be in our parishes, see "What Are We Providing" in the "Hands-On Helps" at the end of this chapter.

Parish leaders sometimes lament that parishioners do not come or respond to opportunities offered at the parish. An advantage to using the above activity as one of the tools in our planning efforts is that we are responding to the felt needs of the parishioners. There are times when we can plan what looks like, to us, a wonderful program with great speakers or resources and interesting activities, but the opportunity might be answering questions that no one has. Therefore, no one responds. A basic principle of adult learning is that formation only works when it is responding to the felt needs of the learner.

Another principle that is crucial as we plan for everyday life needs: adult faith formation occurs in all types of atmospheres and through various methods and channels. To reach out to these many and various groups of people (and many more) doesn't necessarily mean scheduling a speaker series for them. What other creative ways are present within our parish community—and in our area—that can reach all adult members?

Realize That Everything We Do Is Formative

As we talked about in chapter 1 (but it's foundational), *Our Hearts Were Burning Within Us* and many practitioners continually remind us, "The Parish Is the Curriculum" (118). Thus, we are challenged to always examine—and reexamine—everything that happens in parish life—to determine all the ways our life together is affecting and deepening faith.

Let's look at one concrete example: prayer forms. In that simple sentence we could be referring to the many methods and types of prayer. Or we could be recalling the reality that prayer influences and shapes us, forms us. Certainly the main reason for prayer is to praise God, to deepen our union with God. At the same time, how we pray, the environment in which we pray, everything about prayer forms who we are (as individuals and as a community).

Adult faith formation is about formation and transformation. The prayer that happens when we gather "forms" us as much as the meeting, presentation, or conversation. Who we are is how we pray. How we pray is who we are.

What are we forming people for during our prayer, by our prayer? Explore this reality with some of the following questions:

- ✓ Is prayer a part of every adult formation gathering? Is prayer a part of every gathering at the parish? (If it's not, that in itself is teaching people something.)
- ✓ Do we give prayer sufficient time, or do people get the feeling that prayer is something to "be done and gotten out of the way"? (As important as the Lord's Prayer and the Hail Mary are, a hurried recitation of these prayers is usually not adequate for community prayer and reflection.)
- ✓ Do our prayer times incorporate and convey a theologically sound image of God?
- ✓ Do we provide parishioners with a variety of prayer experiences since our faith has a rich tradition and heritage of prayer forms? People with different learning styles, various spiritualities, varying theologies, will enjoy praying in different ways.

Infuse Formation into All That Is Already Happening

New programs, processes, and resources—to meet the discerned needs—are always important. At the same time, notice where and when adults already gather; what procedures and practices of parish life already touch people's lives? How can these opportunities also become moments of formation? Can we consciously include (infuse) study and reflection within these existing activities?

Make a list of the leadership groups and organizations that meet at the parish: parish pastoral council, commissions and committees, parent groups, finance council, ministry teams, liturgical ministers, men's group, women's group, senior groups, small faith communities, and so forth. Then, how do we decide what to use for formation? The parish staff or adult formation committee might select a common resource for all groups to use in an upcoming year. The topic might flow from needs in the life of the parish. Consider these possibilities:

liturgical renewal for a parish preparing for a new worship space
stewardship to support a parish goal for increased ministry involvement
    and fiscal responsibility
church/community for parishes dealing with demographic changes or
    church clustering/pastor sharing

The staff and/or the adult formation team might work with each group, helping them identify topics and find materials related to the specific goals and needs of their group. For instance, a service/social justice commission might explore church social teaching, while a seniors group might study the spirituality of growing older.

These resources might include articles or short excerpts from books that are read prior to the meeting or short videos viewed at the beginning of the gathering—each followed by conversation for the first twenty or so minutes of the meeting. This practice would mean that for any type of meeting, for example, an update for lectors, eucharistic ministers, ushers, the agenda would include not only the logistics of the ministry but also time for formation, for learning more about the Eucharist or Scripture, or for reflection on the meaning of ministry.

Another approach used by many parishes is "Question of the Week." All groups meeting at the church during the week—as well as all households within the parish—reflect on and discuss the same question(s) flowing from the Sunday Scripture readings. These questions could be on a prayer sheet for those meeting at the parish; in the church bulletin and on the website to use at home; mentioned—and encouraged—during the Sunday homily since they flow from the weekends' Scripture readings.

Another way to include infusion is to use every possible method of learning:

+ Enclose a three-minute reading in every parish mailing, in every letter to parents, in any newsletter being mailed to specific groups within the parish, such as ushers, lectors, eucharistic ministers, various committees, shut-ins, etc.

+ Leave small booklets/pamphlets/articles in the gathering space and in the areas where people are waiting to see the pastor/staff.

+ Include the following in the Sunday bulletin and on the website:

   ✓ Short one-liners (or three-minute readings) to answer a question, quote a church document, explain Scripture, pose a reflection question, or suggest a justice and peace action

   ✓ A daily devotion, prayer, Scripture reading, or short quote (changing it often on the website)

   ✓ Short but timely formational information about the church seasons or various issues related to the Creed, prayer, etc. A few possibilities could be: What does the word "Advent" mean? How do we celebrate Halloween as Christians? Why is Good Friday called good?

What's in the bulletin and on the website—and what's not in the bulletin and not on the website—teach a great deal.

Another approach for infusion is the service opportunities of the parish. Some people, for various reasons, are not attracted to participating in adult formation programs, but are very willing to volunteer to be of help, especially in service to others. They will contribute to and work with the Advent Giving Tree, volunteer for Habitat for Humanity, drive people to weekend services, work with Meals on Wheels, read to the blind, visit shut-ins and parishioners in hospitals, work at a homeless shelter or soup kitchen, and so on. Being involved in living discipleship, of course, is the best form of adult formation there is! "Adults do not grow in faith primarily by learning concepts, but by sharing the life of the Christian community. Not that concepts are irrelevant; they are foundational. But for most people the truths of faith really come alive and bear fruit when tested and put into practice—in soup kitchens, neighborhoods, small groups, workplaces, community organizations, and family homes. Adult catechesis practitioners need to learn to tap the learning potential of these diverse settings of Christian ministry and daily life" (*Our Hearts Were Burning Within Us*, 83).

What can we do to enhance the service experience for adults, so that it deeply touches their lives, not only the lives of those they serve? John Dewey reminds us, "We do not learn from experience; we learn from reflecting on experience." Hence, how do we provide time after the service experience for reflection and conversation on questions such as: How did you meet Jesus? How will your life be different because of this experience? In this process of action—followed by reflection and conversation on what happened—deep formation happens!

There are many challenges—and exciting possibilities—in adult faith formation, especially as envisioned by our church documents. It may take thirty (or many more) years for us to entirely implement the vision of *Our Hearts Were Burning Within Us*, but let us believe that it will happen as we continue on the road. In the book *The Hundredth Monkey*, Ken Keyes Jr. tells of a phenomenon observed by scientists when they studied the eating habits of macaque monkeys. One monkey discovered that by washing sweet potatoes before eating them, they tasted better. She taught her mother and friends until one day a certain number (say 99) of the monkeys knew how to wash their sweet potatoes. The next day, when the hundredth monkey learned how to wash sweet potatoes, an amazing thing happened: the rest of the colony miraculously knew how to wash their potatoes too! Not only that, but the monkeys on neighboring islands also all started washing their potatoes.

Reflection/Conversation Starters

📖 As we look at our adult faith formation offerings, which ones form people for membership in the church and to be prophetic Christians in service and mission to the world?

📖 What is already happening in our parish that helps people to grow in faith and discipleship?

📖 As we think of the practices, programs, procedures, and guidelines in our parish, what do people "learn" from them?

📖 How are our parishioners being formed by the prayer times that occur in each gathering at the parish?

📖 What steps might we have to take to introduce a short time for formation at every parish gathering?

📖 How are our Sunday bulletin and parish website offering formation—in addition to information?

📖 What's not on our website and not in our bulletin? What might that be "teaching"?

📖 How and when have we invited adults to reflection and conversation concerning their participation in service? How might we do it in the future?

Hands-On Helps

🕊 See Janet Schaeffler, "Some Practical and Concrete Things to Begin Doing Right Away in 'Beginning' Adult Faith Formation," http://www.janet schaeffler.com/Some_Things_to_do_right_away.pdf.

🕊 See Schaeffler, "What Are We Providing," http://www.janetschaeffler .com/Lens_of_Everyday_Life_Needs.pdf.

🕊 For some practical ideas of prayer in the parish, see issues 45, 53, 60, and 71 of *GEMS: Great Endeavors Mined & Shared*, http://www.janetschaeffler .com/Best-Practices.html.

🕊 To explore a prayer idea for the whole parish—which takes place in the households of the parish—see Schaeffler, "It Happens at Home," *GEMS: Great Endeavors Mined & Shared* 50 (February 2015), http://www.janet schaeffler.com/GEMS__50.pdf.

5

A Royal Welcome
Out of the Ordinary Hospitality

Do not neglect hospitality, for through it some have unknowingly entertained angels.

—Hebrews 13:2

In the September 12, 2011 issue of *America* magazine, Jay Cormier, adjunct professor at St. Anselm College, Manchester, New Hampshire, recounts his experience of teaching the freshman religion seminar. In spending the semester with these students, he realized, "Religion is not so much about believing as it is about belonging." In a reflection paper on "what parable of Jesus did you find most meaningful?" more than half wrote about Jesus' admonitions on not judging others. Jay realized that this generation values acceptance, respect, welcoming. The students were asked to design the "perfect" church setting. Jay was expecting modern art and entertainment. "But what the students valued above all else was being welcomed, feeling that they had something valuable to contribute."[1]

It's not just young adults. The stories abound. On a website that is no longer active (Site Organic: Websites the Way God Intended), there was this account: "Sadly, it is this issue of welcome that frequently breaks down. In a recent survey of people who stopped attending church after several months, 92 percent of them said it was because no one talked to them."

Years ago I began thinking about the importance of hospitality in adult faith formation settings, but quickly realized that it was much more than that. Chapter 3 mentioned that one of the signs of a vibrant parish—which sets the foundation for adult formation—is an innate spirit of invitation and hospitality. Why should we be concerned about this? Perhaps the core reality is that it's who we are; it's how we're made if we're Catholic Christians. An "individual Christian" is an oxymoron. The unique thing about the Christian religion is that we aren't called by God as individuals. It's never just about me and God.

The Second Vatican Council said, "God did not create people to live as individuals but to come together in the formation of social unity, so he 'willed to make women and men holy and to save them, not as individuals without any bond between them, but rather to make them into a people' . . . This solidarity must be constantly increased until that day when it will be brought to fulfillment" (*Gaudium et Spes* 32).[2] Thus, welcoming/hospitality is integral to who we are. The Scriptures and Vatican II remind us that we are the Body of Christ; we are created as one.

Just What Is This Practice of Hospitality?

At times, perhaps, we presume hospitality is the added little touches that we do, the extras to make things a little warmer and friendlier. It is much more than that. It is the bedrock, the grounding of everything.

The welcome that is extended and portrayed in everything a parish does is a reflection of the theology of the parish. The wise and ancient proverb "What you do speaks so loudly that I cannot hear what you say" rings especially true when it comes to how we live and what we do day-by-day in parish life and how that welcomes people (or turns them away). Everything that happens in parish life (and beyond) is rooted in its theology and spirituality of welcome and hospitality.

Often, too, we speak of welcome in relationship to the newcomer, the visitor, and the seeker. Certainly this is crucial (a good exercise is to look at all we do through the eyes of someone who is coming to the parish for the first time). Yet, hospitality/belonging extends to all: the newcomer who may never return again, the registered parishioner of fifty-six years, the active parishioner who has served in every ministry of the parish, the parishioner who is always there for liturgy but has never been actively involved in other areas of parish life, the five-year-old squirmy youngster, the ninety-three-year-old who is hard of hearing, singles, families, couples, widow(er)s, the divorced, separated, and remarried (just for starters).

We're All Responsible

Another usual presumption is that the pastor and pastoral staff are responsible for the parish's hospitality. They are certainly extremely important. The staff can set the atmosphere and has the potential for calling forth the best from parishioners. Yet, the staff does not have sole responsibility. It is their role to call everyone to be welcomers, to build parishes that are hospitable, inviting, and welcoming.

A look at our history is revealing. Welcoming/hospitality became, rightly so, a parish focus in the 1990s. We hosted newcomer gatherings; ministers of hospitality were installed; we encouraged ushers to brush up on their hospitality skills. Did that have an unfortunate consequence? It's possible that it caused the rest of us to see greeters and ushers as "owning" the ministry of hospitality. Have many of us continued interacting only with those we know? Whose "job," then, is the ministry of hospitality in a parish? Perhaps the real question is, has welcoming/hospitality been reduced to a "ministry of hospitality" or are our parishes hospitable communities—because each and every person is living inclusivity, welcoming, and hospitality?

Likewise, not only is every person responsible for welcoming, but every person needs to feel welcomed. There are horror stories of people belonging to a parish for twenty-five years and no one ever talking to them. How does that happen? Stories of people sitting in the same pew for thirty-five years; then they're not there any longer and no one notices. That is not of the Gospel. Welcoming/hospitality is for all and directed toward everyone.

Hospitality In and Within Adult Faith Formation

One of the first foundations for adult faith formation in a parish, then, is that everything about the parish needs to exude a welcoming environment. Without this, very few parishioners—and visitors—will be interested in adult faith formation. It won't be necessary to even plan for hospitality *in* adult faith formation unless parishioners first have a sense of belonging *to and within* the parish. Neil Parent, former executive director of the National Conference for Catechetical Leadership, says in *A Concise Guide to Adult Faith Formation*, "When it comes to perception, a parish that exudes warmth, hospitality, and friendliness will have an easier time attracting parishioners to its programs. And that removes one more motivational hurdle."[3]

In a survey of 144 parishes that I did in 2006, the following were the main components that came to people's minds about hospitality within adult faith formation (including the times mentioned): refreshments, sometimes a meal (119); icebreakers, greeting those nearby, conversations (17); greeters (10); comfortable environment (7); name tags (6); a setting other than the parish (5); personal invitation (5); welcoming facilitator (5); time for food and socializing before and/or after the gathering (5); attention to beauty—table-cloths, centerpiece, etc. (3); printed materials (3); good signage (2); keeping to the time frame (2); sacred prayer area (1); inviting and engaging website (1); hospitality within the life of the parish (1). From this—as well as from many articles on hospitality within adult faith formation—it's easy to see that welcome and hospitality encompass many and various realities.

Hospitality in Refreshments

Let's first explore the one that comes to mind most often; we don't have to go far to see its universal importance. In a book that every adult formation minister would find beneficial, *Community: The Structure of Belonging*, Peter Block says, "In creating the conversation and social space that supports community, another dimension of welcome is what has traditionally defined culture: food. It brings the sacred into the room. It is the symbol of hospitality. It is as direct as we can be about a life-giving act. When we take it seriously, we know how to do this right. What is needed is consciousness about having food and what kind of food fits our intention."[4]

Can what chef Art Smith says in *Back to the Table* about families apply also to communities gathered for adult faith formation? "This sense of security is underscored when a family regularly comes together for meals. When I hear laughter erupt in a quiet dining room, I know I am home free. Eating a meal together is almost magical—and creating this magic gets easier the more you do it."[5] Through the lens of ministry, listen to Fr. Michael Papesh in *Good News Parish Leadership*: "Following from the pattern of life Jesus has shown us, the central place of hospitality in gospel ministry suggests that food and drink should be the largest single budget item for any parish community. To be church together requires our eating and drinking together. . . . The experience of food and drink, hospitality at every parish event ought to be a commonplace, ordinary, expected, most gracious, and downright lovely . . . always, without exception."[6]

These actual practices from parish leaders and adult faith formation committees can spark ideas for us:

> "A light supper was important since the event began at 6:00 p.m."
>
> "We had food that coincided with the theme (food that would have been used in Paul's time: pita, hummus, olives, cheese, etc.)."
>
> "Refreshments (in home groups) were designed to draw people in, i.e., the scent of freshly popped corn or baking cookies . . . things that help people feel at home and comfortable."

"Hospitality has been different each month depending on the topic or season of the year."

"We like to keep it healthy, heart-healthy, if possible; food for the various ages of the group."

"We had afternoon tea afterwards, joining with an activities group which was already having tea in the centre" (from an Australian parish).

"We use real glasses and dishes, tablecloths and table skirts for the serving tables."

Hospitality within Meeting Spaces

Imagine this scene: The adult formation coordinator invites fourteen parishioners to a gathering to discuss the formation of an adult faith formation team. The only facility available for the meeting is a second-floor classroom (no elevator) with desks for seventh-graders, florescent lights, glass block windows, and the lingering smell of chalk dust and pencil shavings.

If this were to happen, what might it "say" before the conversation ever began? The spaces and places for adult faith formation and the creation of hospitable environments are an integral part of hospitality. "Physical space is more decisive in creating community that we realize. Most meeting spaces are designed for control, negotiation, and persuasion. While the room itself is not going to change, we always have a choice about how we arrange and occupy whatever room we are handed" (Peter Block, *Community: The Structure of Belonging*).[7]

When adults host others in their homes, they know how to make others feel welcomed and comfortable. All that is needed in those occasions of welcome and warmth is also necessary for adults in a learning situation: comfortable seating and adult furnishings, rooms available for large and small groups, peaceful and attractive surroundings, handicap accessible buildings and gathering spaces, adequate restroom facilities, a high-quality sound system, good lighting, temperature control and sufficient ventilating.

We know that adults continue to learn; learning certainly does not end with the end of adolescence. What might change, however, are the physical comfort levels. Children and youth might be oblivious to some things that adults notice right away and absolutely need. A friend of mine recounted her recent experience: "Last night I began teaching a Scripture course. We meet in the new parish library, a lovely space built in the round, with large windows, cheerful paint, space for a prayer table, and is entered through a lovely courtyard. However, the furniture is 'temporary' until there are 'more funds.' So, adult bodies were sitting on metal folding chairs for two hours. I told them that this was enough penance for the whole of Lent. No need to do any more. They laughed! A member of the parish council is in the class. I think he will ask for better chairs . . . We shall see!"

The renowned author Parker Palmer, in *A Hidden Wholeness: The Journey Toward an Undivided Life*, suggests, "We seem to have forgotten that the environment in which we meet has an impact on the quality of what happens within us and between us. Fortunately, there is a simple formula for a setting that welcomes the soul . . .

- ✓ Let the room be neither cramped nor cavernous, with enough space to allow for a circle of comfortable chairs that (if the group is large) can easily be moved and gathered into small groups.
- ✓ Let there be eye-level windows to provide visual relief and allow the outside world to come in.
- ✓ Let the decor be warm and inviting, with simple grace notes such as fresh flowers.
- ✓ Let there be carpet on the floor so the sound does not bounce around and acoustics that permit soft voices to be heard by all.
- ✓ Let the lighting be incandescent and warm, not florescent and cold."[8]

Parker Palmer's vision is, perhaps, the ideal. We know that not *all* things are possible, but *some* things are *always* possible. Here are some options to ponder:

- ✓ Are there spaces and places that you can enhance for adult gatherings? How?
- ✓ Do you have a subcommittee (of the adult formation committee) for environment?
- ✓ Does part of your environment always include a prayer space?
- ✓ Do people feel they are entering a sacred space, a welcoming space, a place of comfort and respect?

Qualities/Characteristics of a Hospitable Environment

Malcolm Knowles, a leader in adult education, said in *The Modern Practice of Adult Education*, "I see the setting of a climate that is conducive to learning as perhaps the single most critical thing I do as a facilitator of learning."[9] The physical spaces and places that we just explored are crucial. At the same time, many intangible characteristics (or the social environment) will pervade an adult faith formation setting that is built on the groundwork of hospitality. The following are a few of the many intangible qualities:

Safety and confidentiality: Adults will be confident in a setting in which they feel secure; in which they know their opinions, thoughts, and questions will "stay there"—they will not be repeated or discussed outside of their learning space.

Inclusivity: Usually within an adult faith formation gathering there is a broad range of participants: various ages, many cultures, different needs, and so forth. Facilitators of adult formation are aware of this, for as soon as someone feels excluded in any way, adult learners will begin to lose motivation and enthusiasm.

Respect for each individual: Adult faith formation is not about workshops, courses, classes, and various topics. Adult faith formation is about accompanying people on the walk of faith. It is about being open to God: God within me; God within each and every person. We are on sacred ground together.

Acceptance: To create an environment of hospitality, all participants must feel that questions are OK here; all topics can be discussed; opinions, insights, and experiences are respected. "It needs to be an environment where persons can express anger and doubt without being judged; it needs to be a place where persons can speak without embarrassment about how God has touched their lives" (Linda J. Vogel, *Teaching and Learning in Communities of Faith*).[10]

Attitude of the facilitator: Many years ago (405 AD), St. Augustine wrote a treatise on catechesis, *De Catechizandis Rudibus*, in which he encouraged adult catechists to exude joy in their ministry. People listen to us with much greater pleasure when we ourselves take pleasure in this work.

Some Suggestions and Methods for a Hospitable Environment

Flowing from these characteristics, there are several practices that lay the foundation for a hospitable environment. The song that was No. 1 in 1954 and was in the Top 40 again in 1960, "Little Things Mean a Lot," rings true. Even though some of the following practices might *seem* little and unimportant and thus, we think, for the sake of time they can be skipped, we might want to think again.

Name tags: It is often easier to begin a conversation with someone when you can call them by name. An alternative to name tags is name cards on the tables in front of each person. An advantage is that the names can be much larger, therefore, easier for the facilitator and other participants to read.

Greeters: Often we think of greeters for liturgies, but wouldn't they also lend much to an adult formation gathering? Some parishes have used young adults, the adult faith formation committee, the education commission, or different volunteers each week. Don't limit greeters to only the beginning; as people are leaving, a casual but interested "hope to see you again" increases their sense of belonging.

Icebreakers: Introduction exercises (when they're done well) are not gimmicks or time-fillers. They are an opportunity to emphasize that each person is important and unique, that the facilitator (and the participants) is interested in each and every person. It is easier to learn together, to grow in faith together, when we know something about each other.

Group Guidelines: Depending upon the nature and length of the adult faith formation offering, the facilitator and the group may want to agree to participation guidelines. Here are some that might be considered:

> Listen respectfully, especially to differing perspectives.
>
> Keep personal information shared in the group confidential.
>
> Speak from your own experience, e.g., "I think . . ." or "In my experience I have found . . ." rather than "People say . . ." or "We believe . . ."
>
> Express perspectives without blaming or scapegoating.
>
> Avoid generalizing about people or groups of people.
>
> Don't monopolize.

Reflection/Conversation Starters

- Do we (parish staff, parish pastoral council, commissions, adult faith formation committee) realize that all the facets of parish life have the potential to be welcoming?
- What is our parish's theology of welcoming? How is it practically lived out?
- Do the parish staff, the parish council, and the commissions regularly evaluate the procedures, buildings, activities, etc., of the parish through the lens of welcome and belonging?
- How would newcomers feel if they called our parish? if they participated in liturgy? if they attended an adult faith formation offering?
- Does our theology and practice of welcome become so focused on the newcomers and the returning members that we forget to nurture and appreciate those who are always present?

📖 What's our parish's attitude toward the "infrequent visitors"—those who might participate only on Christmas and Easter?

📖 Who did Jesus spend most of his time with, outsiders or insiders? What about us? Are we limiting "pastoral care" to only those inside our parish membership?

📖 How does our parish build bridges of care to the whole neighborhood around us? Name some specific ways.

📖 Where are the "entry points" for newcomers to our parish? Are there "nonthreatening" activities that are relatively easy for them to take part in on a regular basis?

📖 With what words might parishioners and visitors describe our adult faith formation sessions as hospitable? Are there other areas of hospitality within our gatherings to which we might need to be attentive?

Hands-On Helps

🐚 Barbara J. Fleischer, *Facilitating for Growth* (Collegeville, MN: Liturgical Press, 1993).

🐚 For more reflections and ideas on welcome/hospitality within the life of the parish, see issues 3–9, 46–49, and 56–58 of *GEMS: Great Endeavors Mined & Shared*, http://www.janetschaeffler.com/Best-Practices.html.

🐚 To peruse more ideas and practices that provide hospitality in adult faith formation, see issues 15–17 of *GEMS*, http://www.janetschaeffler.com/Best-Practices.html.

Notes

[1] Jay Cormier, "Student Teachers: What I learned from my class about the faith," Faith in Focus, *America*, September 12, 2011, http://americamagazine.org/issue/786/faith-focus/student-teachers/.

[2] Austin Flannery, ed., *Vatican Council II: Constitutions, Decrees, Declarations; The Basic Sixteen Documents* (Collegeville, MN: Liturgical Press, 2014).

[3] Neil Parent, *A Concise Guide to Adult Faith Formation* (Notre Dame, IN: Ave Maria Press, 2009), 58.

[4] Peter Block, *Community: The Structure of Belonging* (San Francisco: Berrett-Koehler Publishers, 2009), 148.

[5] Art Smith, *Back to the Table* (New York: Hachette Books, 2013), 81.

[6] Michael Papesh, *Good News Parish* (New London, CT: Twenty-Third Publications, 2008), 42.

[7] Block, *Community*, 151.

[8] Parker Palmer, *A Hidden Wholeness: The Journey Toward an Undivided Life* (San Francisco: Jossey-Bass, 2004), 85.

[9] Malcolm Knowles, *The Modern Practice of Adult Education* (Englewood Cliffs, NJ: Cambridge Book Co., 1988).

[10] Linda J. Vogel, *Teaching and Learning in Communities of Faith* (San Francisco: Jossey-Bass Publishers, 1991), 104.

6

Why Should I?
Motivation for Adult Faith Formation

O ne of the predominant questions discussed by adult formation ministers is, how do we motivate adults to grow in their faith? Terrel Bell, the Secretary of Education in President Reagan's cabinet, once said, "There are three things to emphasize in teaching: The first is motivation, the second is motivation, and the third is (you guessed it) motivation."

A challenging thought was on the former website for the Nebraska Institute for the Study of Adult Literacy: "Motivation is an unstable hypothetical construct which cannot be directly measured." Then it went on to explain:

✓ "People have a finite amount of energy that can be applied to a goal.

✓ People change their minds about what they want.

✓ They vary in how they feel—at different times.

✓ They vary in how much effort they will expend when they finally get to it.

✓ Friends, family, job, sports, normal life, all compete with education."

Edward Deci and Richard Flaste in *Why We Do What We Do* pose an important consideration: "The proper question is not, 'How can people motivate others?' but rather, 'How can people create the conditions within which others will motivate themselves?'"[1] Thus, our real question is, how do we motivate to motivate?

With that in mind, there has been much research about adult learning and motivation. Leon McKenzie and Travis Shipp, at the time two professors at Indiana University, were perhaps the first to seriously study reasons for participation in adult *religious* education. Even though their research took place in the early 1980s, today's statistics would likely be similar.

Resistance to education: 16 percent had a negative mindset about education (I'm too old to learn; I've learned all I needed; I don't like new ideas, etc.).

Secular orientation: Approximately 13 percent reported they stayed away because they were in some way alienated from church teaching/practice.

Estrangement: Around 10 percent said they felt estranged from the mainstream of the church.

Marginality: 19 percent indicated that they were basically nonjoiners.

Aversion to church-based education: Roughly 18 percent reported that the church-sponsored programs didn't offer anything to meet their needs/interests and they didn't expect to find help through church-based programs.

Activity: 20 percent cited hectic schedules, family or social responsibilities, and/or the programs were scheduled at inconvenient times.

Inability: 4 percent indicated physical limitations as a reason for not participating.

Helping Adults Motivate Themselves

Adult faith formation directors and teams/committees need to address several areas to create the conditions to help people motivate themselves. No one simple motivational formula will work.

The research from McKenzie and Shipp (above) suggests that the character of parish life is a significant influence on motivation (as we took a quick look at in chap. 3). A church that is essentially lifeless, that has uninspiring liturgies and little outreach, is going to have difficulty in engaging adults in ongoing formation. As we just looked at in the previous chapter, a foundational element of parish life is hospitality. If someone doesn't feel a part, doesn't feel at home and comfortable, why would they even want to venture into a deepened journey into their faith—with this community?

An Atmosphere for Motivation

Another implication of the research from McKenzie and Shipp is the need to create an atmosphere that disposes parishioners to learn. Atmosphere includes parish leadership style, financial priorities, the spaces for adult learning, the types of events and gatherings, the visuals (posters, the types of announcements we make, our website, the ways we utilize technology, etc.). All these—

and many others—together proclaim: discipleship warrants lifelong learning and this church takes that responsibility seriously. Is everything we're doing saying that adults are important; adult faith formation is a priority; we've committed to it; we care about our parishioners, as adults? Are parishes—by their very atmosphere—places where it would be difficult not to learn? Does everything about our parish shout that we're a learning community, that it's fun to grow in faith; it's important to grow in faith; there are many ways to grow in faith?

Parishes need to have an ongoing strategy to help adults make connections between being a disciple of Jesus (formation and transformation) and pursuing a deeper understanding of faith (information). Adults need to be helped to realize that what they learned about their faith as children will not serve them completely in their adult lives, especially in our rapidly changing, complex world of questions and challenges.

We absolutely need to be concerned about faith formation for our children and youth. But if we're putting all our resources and time there, and nothing for adults, what message is that giving? What is that teaching? Might that be "teaching" that our faith is a faith only for children? We know it's not, but what would those actions be "saying"?

The Learning Process as Motivational

The research of McKenzie and Shipp also reminds us that we need to address the adult learning process. If parishioners anticipate that the process and the environment will not be meaningful to them, they will not show up (or take advantage of individual and/or online opportunities). Although some will be satisfied with just getting information, the majority of adults are looking for an integrated experience that deepens their faith. High-quality formation integrates prayer, community building, learning, critical analysis, reflection, and conversation. All of these combine to help the formation and transformation happen, to help adults answer the "so what?" question. What does this have to do with my life? Now what? What do I do now?

The research also suggests that even with a good church environment and a well-developed positive orientation to learning, motivation to participate—through many and varied delivery systems—may still be problematic. The growing complexity of adult life and busy schedules is the reality. There is less time to "attend" programs, to engage with others through various methods. What do we do? One important response: don't fight the schedules.

First (as we looked at in chap. 4), what are the various ways we can infuse formation into all the venues of existing parish life?

Second, how can we encourage and support independent learning, as well as learning in small groups—wherever people are: in their homes, in apartment complexes, at their workplaces, wherever/whenever they can create the places? People don't always have to come to the parish building.

Third, utilize today's technology and the ways of connecting that we've never had before: use the internet for online book clubs, parent support groups, Bible studies, ongoing follow-up with various groups (such as sacramental parents, RCIA, etc.); make our parish websites interactive.

Meeting Needs

We've looked at this previously, but it is most crucial when we're thinking about helping adults to motivate themselves. If opportunities do not coincide with needs and interests, adults will not respond. People are attracted— motivated—usually because of one of two things:

> Adults are facing *life transitions* (raising children, aging parents, first reception of sacraments, job changes, faith questions, etc.).
>
> Adults experience a gap between what they presently understand and are able to do, where they presently are on their life's journey, and a desired goal they've set for themselves (or one that their organization/community/church expects). They recognize the gap; they know they have a need, an interest. In the words of Linda Vogel, in *Teaching and Learning in Communities of Faith,* "Adults are most ready to learn when their current way of being and doing appears unable to solve some problem."[2]

Thus, we begin with who the people are, with their needs and interests. Often we start with our needs and interests; we start with church questions rather than life questions. Sometimes we're giving answers for which the people don't have questions; then we wonder why they don't come. It's not that the church doesn't have answers that guide our faith journey, but people have to be ready to hear. The answers, the "content," have to resonate with their lives, their questions, their needs and interests, or they won't even *be there* to hear.

We need to be open to what is happening in real life. How did/do churches respond to 9/11, the sexual abuse crisis, the Sandy Hook tragedy, the violence of ISIS? (Put in there anything that happens locally, nationally, or internationally that grabs the attention, touches the hearts and concerns of the people.) What do churches do? Perhaps we don't begin by having a class: "The church says . . ." We just open our doors to a safe, comfortable place and let people talk about their fears, their anger, whatever their feelings because of the situation. Then, at some point (it might not be the first week), we ask, "What is there in Scripture and our tradition that will get us through this?" There are church answers to our life questions; there are God answers to our life questions. We reach people when we begin with their feelings, their needs and interests.

Challenges of Motivation

There are questions that most adults voice (or quietly think about) when considering adult formation opportunities in all the various formats offered today:

> Is it worth my time?
>
> Is it relevant?
>
> Will the facilitator model genuine faith?
>
> Will the material and discussions be "too deep" for me?
>
> Will the material and discussions be "too simple" for me?
>
> Will I be put on the spot?
>
> Will the group/the program do what it promises?
>
> Will they really care about me?
>
> Is it worth my effort?

These questions revolve around two realities that are uppermost for today's adults:

> Does this meet my life's needs and questions?
>
> Will I be welcomed and feel comfortable, and will it be worth my time?

Our Hearts Were Burning Within Us emphatically reminds us, "Our programs and ministries must be in touch with people's real circumstances and concerns. Just as Jesus did with the disciples on the road to Emmaus, we must journey with people, listen to them, share our faith, help them to find in the Good News the answer to their hearts' deepest questions, and prepare them to live as Jesus' disciples" (82). Simple, but deep, reasons for motivation!

Another piece of research tells us this: adults today hunger for meaning and have a passionate interest in spirituality. George Gallup Jr. and

D. Michael Lindsay, in *The Gallup Guide: Reality Check for 21st Century Churches*, remind us, "The churches in America . . . face a historic moment of opportunity. Surveys record an unprecedented desire for religious and spiritual growth among people in all walks of life. . . . There is an intense searching for spiritual moorings, a hunger for God. It is for churches to seize the moment and to direct this often vague and free-floating spirituality into a solid and lived-out faith."[3]

Reflection/Conversation Starters

- Would the statistics of McKenzie and Shipp be the same for our parish today? What might be some things we could/should do—if these statistics apply to us?
- What in our parish climate proclaims to the adults that we take adults seriously, that adults and their faith growth are extremely important?
- Are our adults motivated to grow in faith because of the climate in the parish; because all the adults around them are engaged—in some way—in lifelong learning; because in our church it is a fun place to learn?
- Do each of our formation opportunities integrate prayer, community building, learning, critical analysis, reflection, and conversation?
- How do we help adults answer the "so what" question each time we gather for and/or provide opportunities/methods for adult faith formation?
- Which of our adult faith formation programs begin, spring from, the people's life questions? Which of our programs are focused on people's life transitions?
- Which local, national, international events have we responded to through adult faith formation? Which current ones could we respond to?
- How will we motivate people to motivate themselves?

Hands-On Helps

Responding to needs as well as providing an involved learning experience that touches the yearnings of today's adult for a life of deepened faith provides the framework to help adults motivate themselves. The church has wisely guided us in what and how to provide faith formation. One of the predominant keys suggested by the church is that the catechumenate is the inspiration for all catechesis. See Janet Schaeffler, "The Catechumante as Model, *GEMS: Great Endeavors Mined & Shared* 33 (September 2013), http://www.janetschaeffler.com/GEMS__33.pdf, for some ideas for what this means and practical suggestions for carrying it out.

Notes

[1] Edward L. Deci and Richard Flaste, *Why We Do What We Do: Understanding Self-Motivation* (New York: Penguin Books, 1996), 10.

[2] Linda J. Vogel, *Teaching and Learning in Communities of Faith* (San Francisco: Jossey-Bass Publishers, 1991), 67.

[3] D. Michael Lindsay and George Gallup Jr., *The Gallup Guide: Reality Check for 21st Century Churches* (Loveland, CO: Group Pub., 2002).

7

A Broad Focus of Exploration

Some Reflections on the Content of Adult Faith Formation

As mentioned in chapter 2, in *Our Hearts Were Burning Within Us* (88–96), the US bishops categorize the six tasks of catechesis, giving us content areas for a comprehensive formation into life as disciples of Jesus Christ: "Knowledge of the Faith" (doctrine, teaching, Scripture); "Liturgical Life" (worship, sacraments); "Moral Formation" (morality, justice, lifestyle); "Prayer" (devotion, contemplation, retreats); "Communal Life" (strengthening relationships); "Missionary Spirit" (living and spreading the Good News).

What Is the Point of Adult Faith Formation?

As mentioned in chapter 1, surveying some of the offerings in any given parish, we might draw the conclusion that adult formation is primarily designed to support adults in their ministry within the church and/or provide formation prior to a new beginning (parents of children preparing for sacraments, couples preparing for marriage, etc.). These two focuses of adult faith formation are extremely important. At the same time, the documents of today's church *call us to more*. The research on motivation for adult learning, challenging us to intentional listening to the life stories of each individual, graced by God's everyday presence, *calls us to more*. The various needs present in our diverse world: many cultures, the ever-growing expanse of ages of adults, the vast array of family and life situations, and so forth, *call us to more*.

We are called to connect faith and life. Our call is not just to be Sunday Christians, but to be faith-filled Christians in our everyday lives. Vatican II boldly proclaimed that the greatest heresy of our time is the separation that Christians make between their life in the world and their faith. We are called to mission, called to bring about the reign of God, "a mission in and to the world . . . to transform the social and temporal order" (*Our Hearts Were Burning Within Us*, 72). In the words of Cardinal Daniel DiNardo, "You never meet the risen Christ without getting a job."[1]

The "point" of adult faith formation is to engage disciples who connect faith and life, who are on fire with bringing about the kingdom of God in today's world. In the words of Linda Vogel, in *Teaching and Learning in Communities of Faith*, "Religious education that insulates us from the problems and potential of the global village in which we live does not follow Jesus' example."[2]

Each and every offering/process of adult faith formation, then, invites participants to go to the center of what life is always about: What does my faith mean for how I live life today? for how I relate to those around me? to all of God's world? to God? What does faith mean for how we, as a community, make decisions and engage with each other? with those we don't see but upon whom our decisions will have an impact? If this is the ultimate "point" of adult faith formation, it must be tended to in many ways: in the processes used, the varied formats employed, and certainly the "content" of our offerings.

Informing, Forming, and Transforming

The purpose of adult formation is to inform, form, and transform.

Faith formation *informs* when we share and pass on the heart and meaning of the Gospel message and the tradition of the church:

- ✓ What methods and opportunities do we use to *inform* adults of the heart of the Gospel and the church's tradition?
- ✓ What aspects of church teaching are covered well through our adult formation opportunities as well as through the life of the parish?
- ✓ What aspects of church teaching might need more attention?

Faith formation *forms* when—through various ways—people develop a relationship with Jesus, when they become followers:

- ✓ What methods and opportunities do we use to *form* adult believers?
- ✓ What aspects of living the faith does our parish do well?
- ✓ Are there aspects of deepening this relationship that need more attention for our parishioners?

Faith formation *transforms* when it enables people to be in continual conversion, when people are empowered to change and transform the world around them:

- ✓ Has our parish life changed, grown, developed as a result of adult faith formation?
- ✓ What methods and events have helped *transform* our parish as a learning community?
- ✓ Because of faith formation, are our parishioners empowered to continue building the reign of God?
- ✓ What are we doing well? Are there things we might do better?

Some Perennial Questions

The following questions, perennial ones—ones we continually ask—are adapted from Jeanne Tighe and Karen Anne Szentkeresti in *Rethinking Adult Religious Education*:[3]

- ✓ What are the faith formation priorities of our parish? Is adult formation among them?
- ✓ Is our parish addressing the "tasks" an adult performs or the "person" an adult is?
- ✓ Why is the notion that all Christians are called to ministry largely unknown—including ministry in the world (as well as parish ministry)?
- ✓ Are we using children's methods to meet adult needs?
- ✓ Is our parish "telling theological-scriptural-liturgical things" to passive listeners seated in rows of metal folding chairs?
- ✓ Are we reluctant to develop "family-centered," "life-centered," "problem-centered" programs?
- ✓ Are we focused on "content development" or on the development of "critically reflective adults"?
- ✓ Do we realize that adult faith formation exists in relationship to a living liturgy, a Christian community, and a community that is always learning?
- ✓ Are parish programs limited to the pastor's time, schedule, and expertise?

Another view of the perennial questions goes beyond the topic of "content," yet is very related to the "content." Tom Zanzig, a consultant in adult spirituality and faith formation, reminds us that each adult is always on a cyclical journey of conversion and spiritual growth:

> Hungers: adults are always searching for "the more."
>
> Search: we are always on a quest to satisfy the hunger; at times the pursuit might be life-giving, at other times it could be death-dealing.
>
> Awakenings: we see, hear, understand things in new ways; these realizations and stirrings are not only intellectual, but can come through all the ways of being human and spiritual.
>
> Response: dependent on many factors (openness, readiness, abilities, etc.), responses will be mixed and varied.[4]

Our very nature of who we are keeps impelling us; we never have it "all done." Each response moves us deeper into our hungers and the cycle continues. Thus, one of our foundational perennial questions will always be, Does each and every adult faith formation opportunity, everything we do as a parish, help and support adults in this cyclic journey of conversion?

Some Annual Questions

The perennial questions (above) are questions that adult formation committees continually ask, striving to meet the everyday life and faith needs of adults. These perennial questions challenge us to be inclusive and integrated, to pastorally envision two-to-four-year strategic plans for adult faith formation rather than "flashbulb" adult faith formation projects, for example, a four-week Scripture series here, a three-week series on prayer there. Vision and goals allow us to have a comprehensive, cohesive plan. What will be the programs and processes that will fit together rather than scattered programs plopped in at the last moment?

At the same time, there are annual questions that need to be at the forefront of planning and content. This might seem contradictory (but it's not); because of our rapidly changing world, adult faith formation planners need to be able to adapt, within their long-range plans, to changing conditions while not losing focus or vision. Annual questions help us to do that. Adaptive planning, tweaking our integrated long-range plan, is a necessary step if we're going to be open and ready to meet the needs that arise and surprise us. Our long-range plan—necessary as it is—can't be set in stone; conditions change (and often overnight!).

Being awake to the annual questions challenges us to be aware of all that is happening around us, realizing that in the real-life happenings dwell the greatest moments of learning and transformation. What do we do in occurrences such as these to engage everyone in learning, conversation, prayer, and formation? Consider how to respond to the following:

> anniversaries and commemorations within the church, our country, and/or the world (the anniversary of Vatican II, a parish anniversary, Hiroshima, etc.),
>
> the death or transfer of a pastor,
>
> tragedies in the community (fire; suicide; sudden deaths, especially of children),
>
> books and movies: those currently capturing the interest of adults, both religious and popular.

One prime example of this was evidenced in a parish in which I ministered. Within a two-month period, the parish grieved the deaths of five children. We had several adult formation gatherings already scheduled for the coming months. We cancelled most of them, designing new opportunities—presentations and times for conversation—to reflect on why bad things happen to good people, healthy ways of grieving, and ways to reach out to those who are suffering/grieving. As in all adult faith formation, the ways and methods used to address these life events, these "annual questions," are multiple: individual study, workshops, retreats, online learning, and so on.

The Possible Expanse of "What Content Is Appropriate?"

Years ago, theology and religious education teacher Gabriel Moran reminded us, "Since all life is sacred, all learning is religious."[5] In *Christian Life Patterns*, psychologist Evelyn Whitehead and theologian James Whitehead also reaffirm that adult formation includes all areas that enable our growth to be disciples: through baptism all Christians are called to give service in the name of the Lord. All Christians are ministers. All the baptized are challenged to strengthen the Body, to build the kingdom, and to live in response to the Word. Growth into Christian adulthood is crucial to this ministry. Adult catechesis, therefore, explores all areas that nurture and affect this growth.[6]

Thus, many leaders in the field of adult faith formation help us to look at the expanse of content for adult faith formation today. Several have suggested that content falls into three categories, because adult formation is about the whole person. Their suggested categories are topics/experiences that (1) are specifically religious or spiritual and relate to church teachings; (2) respond to parishioners' social, economic, and/or health education needs; and (3) build community.

Some people might say that since the goal is the religious development of adults, the content should only include *explicitly* religious content. Does that assume that human development can be compartmentalized, that various aspects of life can be isolated from one another? Is this an example of an artificial separation into the sacred and the secular?

In *The Religious Education of Adults*, adult education professors Leon McKenzie and R. Michael Harton say, "Ideally, religion is coextensive with life. The so-called secular experiences of adults are pregnant with the possibility of religious meaning. . . . When adult religious education concentrates solely on topics perceived as sacred or holy, the implication is that a host of educational needs and interests arising out of daily life are trivial, a sort of second-class reality. What shapes a person's religious response, however, is the totality of his experience and not simply that part of life experience perceived as sacred. Likewise, a person's religious response influences the manner in which he experiences all of life and not just a segment of life designated as sacred."[7] John Elias, a religious education professor, states in *The Foundations and Practice of Adult Religious Education* that the function of churches and parishes is to help determine what areas of adult development need special treatment from a religious point of view.[8] Tighe and Szentkeresti remind us in *Rethinking Adult Religious Education*, "Solid religious education does not attempt to pour God into the experiences of adult life, but rather to assist the Christian adult in recognizing the holy that has always been active there."[9]

These authors and practitioners remind us that adult faith formation, our very life, is about being holy and "whole-ly." Consider these situations:

> When a parish offers English as a second language for immigrants, with the intent to help them live fully functioning, productive, and meaningful lives, that is responding to the religious mandate of the dignity of each human person.
>
> When a parish explores topics such as those raised by the National Issues Forums, the conversations are reflective of adult formation, by virtue of the cultural/psychosocial context and the intentionality of the learners and the facilitators.[10]
>
> When a parish uses RE-TED (Religious Education using TED.com videos), it attempts to connect the resources and wisdom of our culture

with faith life. While most TED Talks are not explicitly religious, the wisdom provided by these speakers comes ultimately from God through their talents, expertise, insights learned from personal experience, and in-depth study.[11]

Content Related to People's Lives and Experiences

The Pew Forum on Religion and Public Life has conducted extensive surveys on religious beliefs and practices.[12] In one of them, of those who left Catholicism for another church, 71 percent said they left the church because their spiritual needs were not being met. Echoing *Our Hearts Were Burning Within Us*, the pastoral instruction on social communication, *Aetatis Novae* (A New Era), challenges, "The Church therefore must maintain an active, listening presence in relation to the world—a kind of presence which both nurtures community and supports people in seeking acceptable solutions to personal and social problems" (8).

In 2006, NCCL (National Conference for Catechetical Leadership) conducted a best practices study (Dave Riley and Jack McBride, *Best Practices in Adult Faith Formation: A National Study*), which found that the number one factor responsible for success in adult formation is attention to what is going on in the lives of adults. "Paying attention to what is going on in the hearts and minds of adults, what is going on in their lives, is crucial and cannot be overstated. This happens in numerous ways both formally and informally. It is not about what we think they need but rather what they say they need" (28). In spite of all that could be taught and the eagerness of the leaders to impart knowledge to learners, events will be dull and uninspiring when answers are given to questions that have not been asked or for which there is no expressed need.

Two of the most successful adult faith formation offerings I experienced were Lenten programs that directly came from the everyday lives of the parishioners. The first we titled "Sometimes I Feel _____; What's a Christian To Do?" Each week we invited a different presenter to explore an emotion/behavior often experienced in our human journey: anger, burnout, loneliness, guilt, difficulty with forgiveness, and fear. Most people participated in all six; some chose specific ones—all to a full-house crowd. The topics chosen allowed presenters—and the conversation of the participants—to focus on everyday realities and feelings as well as explore Scripture and the wisdom of the church and the saints who have gone before us/are still with us.

The second, "Getting to Know Myself Brings Me Closer to God and Others," used the Myers-Briggs Type Indicator (psychological questionnaire) as a tool to highlight an exploration of these topics:

Discovering More about How God Made Me

I'm Not Peculiar; We're Just All Different

Our Strengths and Complementarities in Relationships, at Work, in Decision-Making

Who We Are Is How We Pray

Developing and Growing Because of Our Shadow Side

The Challenge of Lent/Conversion All Year: The Strengths and Diversity of You and I Together

This exploration of our human faith journey led to deeper understanding of Scripture passages, the insights of our tradition, practical ways of continuing growth and conversion, and deepening relationships.

The Prophetic Role in Providing for Adult Formation

Everything constantly reminds us to offer adult formation flowing from the needs of the people (it's been mentioned here in several ways). There may be times when parish leadership, in being faithful to the Gospel, realizes that there are some other issues that need to be explored. Sometimes our views on God, Scripture, holiness, morality and ethics, and spirituality need to be expanded, at times even challenged.

Is there a time and place for providing opportunities that parishioners haven't requested? Is it the role of leadership to raise awareness and consciousness, inviting people to go deeper? There may be issues that today's Catholics need to explore—within a faith context—that they might not initially see as relevant to their everyday lives, such as immigration, universal health care, the gap between the rich and poor, climate change, the death penalty. Finley Peter Dunne, a humorist, coined the phrase "comfort the afflicted and afflict the comfortable." Dunne placed it in the mouth of his character Mr. Dooley, who was talking about the role of newspapers, but it very appropriately describes the role of adult faith formation.

Adult faith formation—as all realities within our faith—is not either/or but always both/and. Responding to the needs and the everyday lives of our parishioners is imperative; at the same time, the Gospel is always challenging. We need to be faithful to Jesus' call to always be more, to be countercultural, to make a significant difference within our society.

Reflection/Conversation Starters

📖 How do our adult formation offerings inform? form? transform?

📖 What perennial questions do we keep before us?

📖 How do we address the annual questions and the spontaneous happenings in the lives of people, the parish and church, our society?

📖 What do we envision as appropriate topics/themes for adult faith formation?

📖 Does our parish accommodate or challenge, enrich or transform?

📖 What topics are people not asking for, but are needed for disciples in today's world?

Hands-On Helps

🐍 For some examples of the possible variety of offerings that fall within each content area given in *Our Hearts Were Burning Within Us*, go to http://www.janetschaeffler.com/AFF-Helps.html, and explore the links under "What Are We Providing for Adult Faith Growth?"

🐍 As an example of the reality that "content" can be explored through many contexts, see Schaeffler, "In the Process is the Growth," http://www.janetschaeffler.com/In_the_process_is_the_growth.pdf.

Notes

[1] Jordan McMurrough, "Use the media well to teach the faith, cardinal encourages Catholic leaders," *Catholic Online*, March 18, 2008, http://www.catholic.org/news/hf/faith/story.php?id=27225.

[2] Linda J. Vogel, *Teaching and Learning in Communities of Faith* (San Francisco: Jossey-Bass Publishers, 1991), 95.

[3] Jeanne Tighe and Karen Anne Szentkeresti, *Rethinking Adult Religious Education* (Mahwah, NJ: Paulist Press, 1986).

[4] Tom Zanzig, "Discipleship and the Lifelong Process of Conversion," http://www.tomzanzig.com/Site/Handouts_files/Conversion%20Notes--Simple.pdf.

[5] Gabriel Moran, *Education Toward Adulthood: Religion and Lifelong Learning* (Mahwah, NJ: Paulist Press, 1979).

[6] Evelyn and James Whitehead, *Christian Life Patterns* (New York: Crossroad, 1992), 26.

[7] Leon McKenzie and R. Michael Harton, *The Religious Education of Adults* (Macon, GA: Smyth & Helwys, 2002), 6.

[8] John Elias, *The Foundations and Practice of Adult Religious Education* (Malabar, FL: Krieger Pub Co, 1993), 91–92.

[9] Tighe and Szentkeresti, *Rethinking Adult Religious Education*, 76.

[10] National Issues Forums, http://www.nifi.org.

[11] See the many posts on RE-TED at the *Good News Ministries* blog, http://gnmforum.blogspot.com/search/label/RE-TED/.

[12] Pew Research Center, *America's Changing Religious Landscape*, http://www.pewforum.org/2015/05/12/americas-changing-religious-landscape/.

8

Oh! The Differences

It's Not Just Your Grown-Up Child

The longer we interact with people, the more we learn and realize the uniqueness of each person. No one is a copy; all are unique. The more we minister in adult faith formation, the more we learn and realize the uniqueness of each adult. There are countless instances of differences: adults learn differently than children; there are multiple, differing ways to learn; people demonstrate the multiple intelligences in unique ways; the various generations see and experience reality differently; because of age, experience, and life situations, adults have differing needs.

And the list could go on and on. We inhabit a universe that is characterized by diversity. The hallmark of any adult gathering is heterogeneity. Adults are more likely to be different than the same. (For example, a group of sixty-year-olds is different than a group of forty-year-olds, and not all sixty-year-olds are the same.)

Adult Faith Formation: Many Possibilities

Let's stop and reflect for a moment (before you continue reading): where do you experience God?

You might have said prayer, Scripture, nature, in/with people, Eucharist, sacraments, music, art, silence, suffering. I would imagine that no one mentioned "speakers, lectures." We need to remember that when we plan adult formation opportunities.

Adult faith formation can be many things—not only a lecture series, but book clubs, service opportunities, support groups, retreats, and so forth. At the same time, adult opportunities need to include all types of activities because people learn—people experience God—in differing ways. One adult faith formation gathering, then, could include as many different activities as possible, the various activities and methods that would be appropriate for the particular theme being explored: silence and reflection; input; sharing and conversation; music, art, drama, poetry, literature; prayer; activity; decision-making for the days ahead.

We also need to look at various types of approaches. *Our Hearts Were Burning Within Us* talks about five approaches: liturgy, home/family centered, small groups, large groups, and individual activities (97–112). In reality—with today's quickly changing world—there are even more than that (or they are subcategories of these five), especially technology and blended approaches (technology as well as face-to-face). As John Roberto, president of LifelongFaith Associates, constantly reminds us, our role is to build an adult faith formation network that encompasses many approaches and methods for those who come to the parish and for those who might not be able to (or won't) come: parish programs, blogs, support groups, mentors, online courses, retreats and activities, programs in the community, video conferences, apps, weekly liturgy, small faith communities, online small groups, online resources, justice and service projects, intergenerational programs, resources for home study, and so on.[1]

Does One Size Fit All?

When I did a best practices study in adult faith formation, one of the questions asked, "Who was your intended audience?" Most answered "all adults" or "the entire parish." More and more research (and practice) indicates that what works is what's planned for "communities of like interest." People have different needs, are at various stages of human development and faith development, are in various transitions in their lives, and have diverse questions.

Nearly a century ago in the business world, Henry Ford invented the famous "assembly line," credited with putting Detroit and the world in the "mass production" business. When he introduced the Model T, the marketing message was essentially, "You can have any color you want as long as it is black." Don Tapscott, author of several books on today's digital world, uses a different term to describe what drives business today: mass customization. In effect, "you can have whatever you want customized to your wishes."

What does this mean for adult faith formation? Often we approach adult faith formation with a "one size fits all" mentality. Yet, the reality is quite different. "Adults will be interested in (and need) different aspects of the religious according to their personal faith development and expression. An approach of corned beef and hash for everyone' (which is tantamount to 'We don't care what you need, this is what you get because this is what we've got') and programs based simply on what the religious educator or pastor wants to teach are too capricious."[2]

We see this graphically illustrated within our parishes: parents of young children need something different than empty nesters; those who have just lost a job have unique needs; people who are new in the faith need something different than those who have been deeply practicing the faith for years. Many parishes report that they have better responses to offerings when they are planned and advertised for specific groups, for communities of like interest, for example, Scripture study for men rather than a generic Scripture study; an offering for parents of young children targets a specific community and will often attract more people than a generic program on parenting.

Certainly, there are times when "mixed groups" are important; we learn from the wisdom and experiences of each other. There are times when we do plan for everyone, for example, a parish mission or retreat, a Lenten program. Yet, even within those, do we advertise differently to each group? Do we plan some things—within the major event—that might attract and meet the specific needs of particular groups? As Seth Godin, in *Small is the New Big*, says, "A product for everyone rarely reaches anyone."[3]

A Never-Ending Range of Topics for Adult Faith Formation

Given the diversity and the various needs of today's adults, the areas for exploration within adult faith formation are unending. Likewise, there is no compartmentalizing our lives. Everything that happens in our daily lives touches our faith. Therefore, the range of topics that can be, might be, and should be explored within adult formation opportunities (using all methods within face-to-face and virtual possibilities) is never-ending. Listed here are *just a few* of the many topics that might flow from the interests and needs of today's adults:

For Those in Early Adulthood (20s–30s)
- ✓ The role of the Spirit in daily decision-making
- ✓ Predictable crisis in adult life, in the faith journey
- ✓ Single today: opportunities and challenges
- ✓ Family prayer

✓ Juggling the rhythms of family life

✓ Christian alternatives in celebrating holidays

✓ When both spouses work

✓ Religion and spirituality rather than religion vs. spirituality

Some real-life examples: Many parishes (and dioceses) respond to the needs of those in their 20s and 30s through Charis Ministries, which offers retreats, leadership development, and formation activities.[4]

The Basilica of Saint Mary, Minneapolis, Minnesota, hosts *Sunday Night Live*, a monthly gathering for those in their 20s and 30s to explore, in a discussion format, various issues of faith and life, such as "Balancing Simplicity and Abundance," "Beyond Career to Calling," and "Materialism and God."

For Those in Middle Adulthood (40s–mid-50s)

✓ Crisis points in marriage

✓ My kids aren't growing up like I did. Help!

✓ Being the church in the world

✓ "Biblical Reflections: Find Yourself in the Stories of the Bible"[5]

✓ Safety in a cyberspace age

✓ Media literacy: Knowing how the media influences (hoodwinks) me

✓ Traits of a healthy spirituality

✓ 9 to 5: Spirituality of work

✓ Women in the church (and society)

A real-life example: The associate pastor of Holy Name of Jesus Church, Henderson, Kentucky, invites parishioners, each Labor Day, to sign up if they would like him to visit their place of work during the coming year. Throughout the year, then, he visits one or two parishioners each week at a time convenient for them. The purpose is not to tour or meet their employer or employees, but to be present in their work setting, asking them, (1) What do you do? and (2) How do you feel about what you do? He writes up the people's reflections in the coming Sunday bulletin in a column titled "The Sunday/Monday Connection."[6] Twice a year the workers are invited to a small-group session to share ideas, discussing the relationship between faith and work.

For Those in Mature Adulthood (mid-50s–mid-70s)

✓ The joys and challenges of intergenerational households

✓ Support for the caregiver

✓ Helping parents deal with life's losses

✓ The joys of grandparenting

✓ Challenges of midlife transitions

✓ Passages of marriage

✓ Reconciliation in daily life

✓ Christian perspectives on everyday medical dilemmas

✓ From success to significance

✓ Growing older without fear

✓ Forgiveness: is it possible?

✓ The empty-nest syndrome

Some real-life examples: Christians from all over the world have explored and supported each other's spirituality in the second half of life through the STM Online: Crossroads (Boston College) course "Autumn Blessings."[7]

Book clubs—for many—respond to the need for belonging, new understandings, and conversation about things that matter. Book clubs can happen face-to-face (at churches, homes, coffee shops, etc.) or virtually.[8]

For Those in Older Adulthood (75+)

✓ Facing losses gracefully

✓ Wisdom—the gift of age: what do I do with it?

✓ Taking stock: finding meaning in later life

✓ Coping with illness

✓ Life after retirement: writing the next chapter

✓ Choosing lifestyle changes in later life

✓ New-old ways to pray

✓ The comfort and challenge of the resurrection

✓ The 12 keys of successful aging

✓ Jesus laughed—do you?

Some real-life examples: A May 2010 article in *U.S. Catholic* advocated for Yellow Banana Schools of Theology in our churches. ("I don't buy green

bananas. I may not still be here when they ripen and turn yellow.") This pro-
posal was precipitated by the realization that most parishes give much time,
resources, and personnel to children, and some to adults, but very little to
the elder generations. These Yellow Banana Schools would be an "endeavor
powered by the urgency of age. The courses, like a ripe banana, should not
only be short but also sweet. . . . Short and interesting. The sweetener would
be the choice of a dynamic, questioning facilitator instead of an answer-
giving teacher or a dull, lecturing scholar. Most courses would run one session,
seldom two, and never three. The curriculum would be determined mostly
by the students themselves, because as we age, our felt needs increasingly
become our real needs."[9]

One helpful activity for the older adult is a life review: a way to intensify
gratitude and leave a legacy. This may be expressed in a variety of ways: writing
memoirs, previewing and assembling photo albums, taping memoirs, creating
art, planting memory gardens, developing family histories or genealogies,
making trips to family homes or pilgrimages to locations of spiritual significance, writing autobiographies or life histories.

Differing Paths on the Faith Journey

Another way of understanding the differences in today's adults is by understanding the reality of spiritual dwellers and seekers. Sociologist Robert
Wuthnow calls the spirituality of the Hebrew people in the wilderness "a
spirituality of seeking" and the spirituality of the Hebrew people who have
settled the land "a spirituality of dwelling." Today dwellers can be described as
those who find comfort in tradition and are basically content with the spiritual
path they have chosen; seekers find comfort in exploring new possibilities and
see themselves "on the way" spiritually but not there yet. Hence, various—and
differing—types of experiences are needed.

Related to this dwelling/searching reality among adults is the increasing
rise of "nones" (those who do not claim any particular communal faith iden-
tity) and SBNRs (spiritual but not religious). Although these two groups
certainly encompass a diversity of individuals and numerous varied reasons
for self-choosing these options, Linda Mercadante (author of *Belief without
Borders: Inside the Minds of the Spiritual but not Religious*) found that, with
those she interviewed, there were some similarities: "The interviewees did not
shy away from discussing their beliefs, but seemed to relish these questions,
take them seriously, and feel it was important for them to consider. Oftentimes

when I asked for clarification or pointed to seeming inconsistencies or undeveloped areas, the interviewee would say with amazement, 'I never thought of that!' and end with a hug and a promise: 'Now you've given me something to think about!' Almost routinely participants thanked me profusely, saying they wished they could have more opportunities to have discussions like this."[10]

Reflection/Conversation Starters

- How can we plan adult faith formation that is other than "speakers"? In "program-type" offerings, how can we use various methods and activities?

- How can we build an adult faith formation network that includes face-to-face and virtual opportunities?

- What is happening through our adult faith formation offerings that is directed toward various "communities of like interest"?

- What other "communities of like interest" in our parish have needs that could be met through various opportunities?

- How can the people within these communities be empowered to be leaders for the offerings/opportunities?

- As we plan an adult faith formation event/gathering, do we think of the multiple intelligences, of right- and left-brain thinking, of the different learning styles? Do we include various types of activities and methods to reach the various ways of learning?

- Which approaches do we use most often? Is there one (or more) that we usually don't use? Are there ways we might use it in the future?

- Looking at the possible topics (above), how will we determine whether these might be of interest, responding to the needs of our parishioners?

- What would be some of the "delivery systems" we could use to involve people in formation around these topics?

- What are we providing for dwellers? for seekers?

- Do our adult formation opportunities engage people in experiencing God or knowing about God?

- Do our adult faith formation efforts include welcoming ways to invite and/or provide for opportunities for "nones" and SBNRs to have the discussions they seek?

Hands-On Helps

🐾 For a look at some of the adult learning principles, flowing from the reality of the uniqueness of the adult learner, see Janet Schaeffler, "How Adults Learn," http://www.janetschaeffler.com/Adult_Learning_Principles__2_.pdf.

🐾 As you reflect on communities of like interest, see Schaeffler, "Girlfriends in God," *GEMS: Great Practices Mined & Shared* 32 (August 2013), http://www.janetschaeffler.com/GEMS__32.pdf, for an (ongoing) event planned specifically for women; and "Don't Be Caught Dead, Plan Ahead," *GEMS* 13 (November 2011), http://www.janetschaeffler.com/Gems__13.pdf, which illustrates an opportunity for those in mature and older adulthood.

🐾 For more ideas regarding diverse topics, see issues 23, 24, and 27 of *GEMS* at http://www.janetschaeffler.com/Best-Practices.html; and "What Are We Providing," http://www.janetschaeffler.com/Lens_of_Everyday _Life_Needs.pdf.

Notes

[1] LifelongFaith Associates, http://www.lifelongfaith.com/journal.html.

[2] Leon McKenzie and R. Michael Harton, *The Religious Education of Adults* (Macon, GA: Smyth & Helwys, 2002), 120.

[3] Seth Godin, *Small is the New Big* (New York: Penguin, 2006).

[4] Chicago-Detroit Province of the Society of Jesus, *Charis: Connect-Encounter-Grow*, http://charisministries.org.

[5] The Rohr Jewish Learning Institute, "Biblical Reflections: Find Yourself in the Stories of the Bible," http://www.myjli.com/index.html?task=courses_detail&cid=30.

[6] Janet Schaeffler, "Best Practice: The Sunday/Monday Connection," *GEMS: Great Endeavors Mined & Shared* 1 (September 2010), http://www.janetschaeffler.com/Gems__1.pdf.

[7] Kathleen Fischer and Ronald Rolheiser, "Autumn Blessings: Spirituality in the Second Half of Life" (online course, Boston College), *STM Online: Crossroads*, http://www.bc.edu/schools/stm/crossroads/courses/autumn-blessings.html.

[8] See Janet Schaeffler, "A Best Practice: A Process for Gathering Parishioners for a Parish Book Study," *GEMS: Great Endeavors Mined & Shared* 14 (December 2011), http://www.janetschaeffler.com/Gems__14.pdf, for a unique process of inviting and gathering adults for a parish book study.

[9] John J. Donovan, "Seniors need some class: Let's have religious ed for our church elders," *U.S. Catholic* 75, no. 5, http://www.uscatholic.org/seniored.

[10] Linda Mercadante, *Belief without Borders: Inside the Minds of the Spiritual but not Religious* (New York: Oxford University Press, 2014), 18.

9

From Bricks to Clicks

*Communications Technology
and Adult Faith Formation*

O ur world has changed. Before there were computers, this was the reality of our lives:

Memory was something we lost with age.

An application was for employment.

A program was a TV show.

A cursor used profanity.

A keyboard was a piano.

A web was a spider's home.

A virus was the flu.

A CD was a bank account.

A hard drive was a long trip on the road.

A mouse pad was where a mouse lived.

The verbs "friending" and "liking" didn't exist.

"'4G' was a parking space."

"The 'cloud' was still in the sky."

Twitter was the sound a bird makes.

"Skype was a typo!"[1]

Communications Technology and Adult Faith Formation

Previously in catechetical ministry, we needed to have a grasp of theology, catechetics, spirituality, learning styles and methods, and administration (among many other areas). Today an understanding and appreciation of the role of communications technology is crucial to ministry: "For the first time since ancient times, we have the perceptual capabilities to see the world, not just as our little corner of the globe, but as an interconnected multidimensional whole. Thanks to digital technology, text, sound, images, and data have all merged into one common language . . . and one common medium. . . . Led by this new way of looking at things, our very perception of the world has changed. . . . Communication is the medium for relationships, community, and culture, so a more efficient or powerful tool of communication results in their restructuring."[2]

The new generation thinks "in hyperlink fashion, learns through participation, makes decisions collaboratively, and accesses their information electronically. We cannot use yesterday's pastoral and catechetical approaches within today's environment without risking a major disconnect."[3] In the past, when we wanted information or when people wanted to gather, we went to a place (bricks): libraries, our parish, etc. For many people today, that's not the first choice. Researchers say that 90 percent of the inquiries that come to a parish come via their webpage, not telephone calls, not personal visits. We've moved from bricks to clicks.

To think about it from just one perspective: There was a large body of research conducted during the 1980s about adult learning. The consensus was that roughly 85 percent of what adults learned then was not in a formal setting, classroom, or lecture hall; and that was ten to fifteen years before the internet. There has been a significant paradigm shift with adult learning today driven by the internet and, since 2007, by the Wiki world (peer-to-peer sharing). If 85 percent was the percentage of informal learning in the 1980s, just think what it would be today—what it will be tomorrow.

That's not to say that adult faith formation (in its broadest sense) should now be only through one delivery system. In reality, it needs to be both/and: both in physical places and virtual places. In chapter 8 we looked at the wisdom and reality of building an adult faith formation network, which would always include face-to-face and virtual realities.

In December 2013 Pope Francis met with the participants of the 26th Plenary Assembly of the Pontifical Council for the Laity under the theme "Proclaiming Christ in the Digital Age." Francis named some important features of contemporary Christian living and gestured toward a balanced engagement with technology. This has been the church's message for a while. Pope Benedict XVI referred to the internet and the world of technology and social media as a "digital continent" in need of "evangelization." He saw promise in this place where women and men, especially the younger generations, gather and spend their time. This virtual place is where the Gospel can also be lived; it can serve as a guide for right social interaction and use of technology.

Pope Francis is continuing the encouragement to Christians of not shying away from technology and social media: "Guided by the Holy Spirit, we will discover valuable opportunities to lead people to the luminous face of the Lord. Among the possibilities offered by digital communication, the most important is the proclamation of the Gospel." Francis also sees modern communication technologies, especially the internet, as resources for reaching out to people, offering them "real reasons for hope."[4]

A recent search through one search engine for "spirituality" produced 40,700,000 websites. That was just "spirituality"; it did not include "church" and all its variations: prayer, Creed, morality, social justice, and a myriad of other topics that touch our Christian life. If people are on the web searching for or in dialogue on matters of spirituality, current events, human values, relationships, social doctrine, family life, workplace morality, the common good, prayer, or whatever else may delight, concern, or bother them, are we there? Who is offering them the wisdom of the Gospel and the rich tradition of the church on the internet?

There have been several places in past chapters where we've mentioned possibilities for communications technology and adult faith formation. Let's explore a few more.

The Power of Connecting

Communications technology enables us to connect in ways we never imagined in the past. Do we use our parish database for marketing, for motivating, for direct appeal to those who might be interested in happenings at the parish or in the community? When we ask the appropriate questions in parish registration, we have the needed information (people's interests, occupations, etc.) in our database to enable us to do many things:

- If we organized a series on "Ethics in the Workplace," who would be the logical participants? We could directly advertise to them.
- Who expressed interest on the parish interest survey in leading a book discussion group, in working with parents preparing for their child's baptism?
- Who might like to participate in an online study group or a face-to-face book club or new Scripture series?

- Can we stay connected with people after an event, encouraging them to continue delving into the topic/area they were exploring?

  For example, a group of parents of young children met for three weeks, talking about faith in the home. A month later when we come across an article or website giving family prayer ideas, it can be emailed to those who attended.

  Last year's RCIA group can be emailed periodic reflections on the Scripture readings, on the sacraments, on being a disciple in today's world.

Websites and Adult Faith Formation

In chapter 7 we reiterated the reality that three purposes of adult faith formation are to inform, form, and transform. Sunday bulletins and websites often inform, sharing the details and information that people desire and need. That is important; yet, in today's world all the vehicles that we use can go beyond informing. We have the ability, and there is a necessity, to continually form and transform. Consider these suggestions related to websites:

- ✓ Are our websites interactive? Are there places and spaces for connection and conversation? Parishioners can ask for prayer, share faith stories, or respond to the question of the week.
- ✓ Are there downloadable articles, frequently asked questions, blogs? Blogs or webpages can list resources where people can act upon newly discovered insights, such as local organizations in need of volunteers.
- ✓ Blogs can be written by staff members as well as invited parishioners to share faith, reflect on a liturgical season, discuss current events in the light of faith, etc.
- ✓ Blogs give parishioners a chance to interact. What if the blog had a question, perhaps one that is changed periodically, e.g., Where did you experience God today? What's your favorite way of praying? How are you celebrating Advent at home?
- ✓ Some parishes have a section on their website inviting people to ask questions they might have about the faith. These questions are then used for future short podcasts.
- ✓ Are podcasts and streaming video available? Is there a video library of homilies, parish events, and adult faith formation speakers?

As we continually update our parish websites, ask, How are we integrating the use of our website into our adult faith formation plan? How is our website an adult faith formation tool in itself (for information, formation, and transformation)? As part of our adult faith formation plan, also consider these questions:

- ✓ How are we marketing adult faith formation offerings on our website?
- ✓ How are we connecting adults to faith formation opportunities on other websites?
- ✓ Do we provide adult formation programming online?
- ✓ Do we provide resources for adults to download?

Other Communications Technologies for Adult Faith Formation

The possibilities are endless. Consider these two examples:

Each Thursday a parish emails to parishioners the Scripture readings for the weekend. In this email no announcements are included, only the Sunday readings (with a link to the parish website). The parish leadership realize that there are a number of people who have given their email to the parish, but are not always present on Sunday. This is a gentle reminder that the parish is there for them and that people gather each weekend for worship.

Another parish emails "A Thought for the Day" (a reflection on the Scriptures of the day) to parishioners who have requested it; it can also be delivered via phone and/or text and included on the website and the parish Facebook and Twitter accounts. This "Thought for the Day" can be written by parishioners—an example of the faithful evangelizing and sharing faith with one another.

Connecting to the Rich Resources

In addition to generating our own content, there are wonderful resources throughout the internet today (as well as some we would want to avoid). In building a faith formation network, we can research and curate these, passing them on to parishioners in various ways. See the following list for some of the many available resources:

online courses, such as Crossroads from Boston College, VLCFF from the University of Dayton, and STEP at Notre Dame;[5]

various online retreats such as "An Online Retreat" through Creighton University and "Online Retreats" through Good Ground Press;[6]

prayer suggestions, such as *Sacred Space, Pray As You Go* , and "Prayer Resources" (*Ignatian Resources*);[7]

Scripture reflections, such as USCCB's Daily Reflections Video and University of Notre Dame's daily Gospel Reflection;[8]

spirituality, such as *Stay Great* and *Dating God*;[9]

resources on Catholicism, such as *eCatholicism* and "Catholic Internet Directories" (Spring Hill College);[10]

walking with those who, in various ways, are searching, such as *Catholics Come Home*, *Divorced Catholic*, and *Busted Halo*;[11]

family and parenting, such as *At Home with our Faith* and "Home Practices" (*Building Faith*);[12] and

Catholic social teaching, such as *Education for Justice* and *Catholic Social Teaching*.[13]

In addition to these topical/themed resources, there are numerous others, of course, that could coincide with the specific programs and/or adult-generations you're working with, such as:

U.S. Catholic Book Club

For Your Marriage

"Celebrate Easter's 50 Days" (*The Word Among Us*)[14]

Consider these ways to share these sites with your parishioners:

✓ The Sunday bulletin, especially listing "Website of the Week"
✓ Links on our own parish websites
✓ Providing magnet bookmarks a few times a year listing several websites
✓ Alerting participants in past programs of new resources available

Virtual Adult Faith Formation

Even though there are distinct advantages to face-to-face formation opportunities, there are also advantages (as well as some drawbacks) to virtual opportunities. As today's adults increasingly utilize communications technology, we—on our journey of deepened faith—need to employ all of its advantages. An option to consider is a face-to-face program at the parish in which the generations are brought together: youth and young adults help and teach seniors the ins and outs of communications technology—email, Facebook, etc.[15]

In addition to the various ideas mentioned above (and in other chapters), think of all the opportunities offered at your parish. Which ones could also be offered online—book clubs, support groups, Scripture study, an exploration of Catholicism, young adult conversations, and so on?

A blended approach may be an appropriate option: combine both virtual and face-to-face opportunities. One parish designed their baptismal preparation program in this manner. One of the original planners commented, "My motivation to begin the group came from an intuition that told me that parents arriving for a one-evening workshop simply could not process the formation we were hoping for them. There seemed to be little table conversation, and much of what went on at the workshop was within the context of a 'teacher-student' methodology. I just didn't see that fitting well with adult faith formation principles."

Thus, parents and godparents were invited to a closed (they and the parish leadership working with this program) online group. During a four-week period, the parents and godparents read three articles on baptism and Christian parenting and then responded to questions posed by the leaders in the online forums. They were encouraged to discuss and converse with each other, their thoughts flowing from their reading and experience. The leaders moderated these discussions, affirming the participants, answering questions, and asking additional questions, inviting the parents and godparents to delve deeper into the gift of baptism and the privilege (and challenges) of Christian parenting today.

A week before the celebration of baptism, the parents and godparents gathered at the parish to meet one another, to pray together, to bring together some of their learnings and feelings concerning this new step in their family life, and to go over any logistics needed for the day of celebration. People greeted one another as friends, even though many of them had never seen one another. There were spirited conversations and a reluctance to have this time end.

One of the leaders commented, "I had two initial concerns: first, that a lack of 'face-time' would not be community building; secondly, that not everyone would have computer access. The community building has actually been above and beyond my expectations. It is truly amazing to me what people will share, and the questions they will ask behind a computer screen. By the end of the five-week online time, we are all friends, looking forward to meeting one another face-to-face at the one on-site session at the parish. As for computer access, I haven't had one problem with that yet."

Through this program, the parents and godparents were invited into much more than would have happened in a single face-to-face meeting. Perhaps, too, a few introverts, who would have been silent in a face-to-face meeting, gained much from being part of this online process.

Some parishes—for various programs—flip the order of the face-to-face and virtual components. They begin with onsite gathering(s) and then continue the ongoing study and conversations online.

Reflection/Conversation Starters

📖 How would we complete this sentence? Communications technology is important in adult faith formation because _____.

📖 What are our questions and concerns, our hopes and dreams, about the use of communications technology in faith formation?

📖 What are some of the benefits of the use of technology for adult learning and faith formation in our parish? What would be some of the challenges?

Hands-On Helps

🐾 Meredith Gould, *The Social Media Gospel: Sharing the Good News in New Ways*, 2nd ed. (Collegeville, MN: Liturgical Press, 2015).

🐾 Clarissa Valbuena Aljentera, *The Parish Guide to Social Media: How Social Networking Can Recharge Your Ministry* (New London, CT: Twenty-Third Publications, 2013).

🐾 For continuing thoughts on communications technology and adult faith formation, see GEMS issues 40, 41, and 70 at http://www.janetschaeffler .com/Best-Practices.html.

🐾 See Janet Schaeffler, "Online Scripture Study," *GEMS: Great Endeavors Mined & Shared* 11 (September 2011), http://www.janetschaeffler.com /Gems__11.pdf, which details one parish's first attempt at online Scripture study and gives some tools and methods of setting up a platform for online groups.

🐾 An entire issue of *Lifelong Faith* is devoted to "Faith Formation and the New Digital Media"; see *Lifelong Faith* 4, no. 1 (Spring 2010), http://www.life longfaith.com/uploads/5/1/6/4/5164069/lifelong_faith_journal_4.1.pdf.

Notes

[1] A portion of this is taken from Thomas Friedman and Michael Mandelbaum, *That Used to Be Us: How America Fell Behind in the World It Invented and How We Can Come Back* (New York: Picador, 2011), 64.

[2] M. Rex Miller, *The Millennium Matrix: Reclaiming the Past, Reframing the Future of the Church* (New York: Wiley, 2004).

[3] Frank Mercandante, *Engaging a New Generation* (Huntington, IN: Our Sunday Visitor, 2012).

[4] Pope Francis, 26th Plenary Assembly of the Pontifical Council for the Laity, December 2013.

[5] Crossroads (Boston College), http://www.bc.edu/crossroads; VLCFF (University of Dayton's Virtual Learning Community for Faith Formation), https://vlcff.udayton.edu; STEP (University of Notre Dame's Satellite Theological Education Program), http://step.nd.edu.

[6] Creighton University, "An Online Retreat," http://onlineministries.creighton.edu/CollaborativeMinistry/cmo-retreat.html; Good Ground Press, "Online Retreats," http://www.goodgroundpress.com/retreats.aspx.

[7] *Sacred Space*, http://www.sacredspace.ie; *Pray As You Go*, http://www.pray-as-you-go.org; *Ignatian Resources*, "Prayer Resources," http://ignatianresources.com/prayer/.

[8] United States Conference of Catholic Bishops, "Daily Reflections Video," http://www.usccb.org/bible/reflections/; University of Notre Dame, "Gospel Reflection," http://faith.nd.edu/s/1210/faith/start.aspx?gid=609&pgid=61/.

[9] *Stay Great*, http://staygreat.com; *Dating God*, http://datinggod.org.

[10] *eCatholicism*, http://www.ecatholicism.org; Spring Hill College, "Catholic Internet Directories," http://www.shc.edu/theolibrary/dir.htm.

[11] *Catholics Come Home*, http://www.catholicscomehome.org; *Divorced Catholic*, http://divorcedcatholic.com; *Busted Halo*, http://bustedhalo.com.

[12] *At Home with our Faith*, https://homefaith.wordpress.com; *Building Faith*, "Home Practices," http://www.buildfaith.org/home-practices/.

[13] *Education for Justice*, https://educationforjustice.org/catholic-social-teaching-resources/; *Catholic Social Teaching*, http://www.catholicsocialteaching.org.uk/principles/faqs/.

[14] *U.S. Catholic* Book Club, http://www.uscatholic.org/bookclub/; *For Your Marriage*, http://www.foryourmarriage.org; *The Word Among Us*, "Celebrate Easter's 50 Days," http://wau.org/resources/article/re6_family_50_days_easter/.

[15] See the touching documentary *Cyber-Seniors: Connecting Generations*, directed by Saffron Cassaday (Toronto: The Best Part, 2014), http://cyberseniorsdocumentary.com.

10

Thinking Outside the Box

Possible Innovative Options for Adult Faith Formation

*A*s I've said throughout the book, people's faith grows continually, in many ways, in all types of places and contexts. With the involvement of a diverse committee/team, with continual evaluations from partici-pants, with ongoing needs assessment including all parishioners, dreams and possibilities of more and more creative ways to meet a wide variety of needs and interests will abound. Here are some ideas to consider.

1. Designate October (or any month that would be best for your com-munity) as Adult Faith Formation Month in your area. Offer a different topic/event in a different parish each night of the month. Be sure to publish a calendar of *all* the events for *all* the people of *all* the parishes—and beyond.

2. Leave your parish to learn. Use your parish bus, rent one, or use your vans and travel. Tour, and expand your horizons. Have you visited all the other churches in your area? Do you know their history? Have you visited the oldest churches in the (arch)diocese, the Catholic churches that might include various ethnic and racial populations, the Protestant churches in your area, Jewish synagogues, mosques? Have you been to your (arch)diocesan cathedral and retreat centers in the area? After your journeys, plan a parish retreat on another type of journey, the inner spiritual journey, "Time to Go Within—Where God Knows Me First."

3. Host a Sunday Sharing Session. Young or old, people who live alone say that Sunday afternoons are the loneliest times of the week. Open a parish meeting room/gathering area for an hour in late afternoon. After someone has read the gospel for the day, invite those gathered to reflect on it in relationship to events/concerns that are happening in the world.

4. Host an art exhibit on faith and God. There may be many parishioners who have artistically portrayed their spirituality and faith in God, through

paintings, drawings, sculpture, or photography. Invite them to share that. The evening/day could be structured in various ways: time for people to meditatively browse, time for the artists to talk about their experiences, an opportunity for all to try their hand at a creative experience, time for prayer, etc.

5. Bring the practical and spiritual together. Parishioners gather at the parish and are provided with a map of a nature walk in your area (even if it's just through neighborhoods with trees and flowers that in our busyness don't usually get noticed), which also includes suitable places to stop (park benches, etc.) to reflect and share experiences. Before beginning, as well as on one of the stops, the leader might share some input and reflections on prayer-walking. After the walk and stop(s), return to the parish for lunch or snacks and sharing of the experience.

6. You don't always need an "expert." Plan your own parish "talk show" for Lent. Invite a panel of parishioners to gather each week to reflect and share stories from their life experience based on the theme of the upcoming Sunday Scripture readings. This would begin the evening, followed with time, of course, for all the participants, in small groups, to share their own stories.

7. Parishioners can be invited to share their faith experiences; in this process of reflecting on and sharing their faith, growth certainly deepens. During Lent, invite fourteen adults to give a personal reflection on the meaning of one of the Stations in their lives. (Doing this each week will involve even more people.) These can be posted on the parish website and/or published in the Sunday bulletin.

8. Publish your own parish booklet of Advent, Lent, and/or Easter reflections for each day of the season—inviting different adults to each write a page. Have a weekly column in the Sunday bulletin titled "My Favorite Scripture Passage," "A Quotation That Has Helped Me," or "The Best Book I've Read This Year" and invite adults to write their personal reflections on how these insightful helps have inspired their lives.

9. Tables for Two is an evening of sharing for married couples and/or engaged couples at a five-course dinner seasoned with guided discussion. The goal is to support couples in continuing development of their enriching relationships. Often parishes schedule this event around Valentine's Day. (This type of format could also be used for Parent and Son/Daughter evenings to give either parent the opportunity to spend a quiet evening of sharing with a teenaged or older son/daughter.)

10. During Lent offer an adult formation "mini-conference" in your parish. Offer three different topics each night for a week. Won't that boost participation?

When only one opportunity is offered, your audience is limited. With three topics to choose from, many more people might be attracted, because their interests/needs are being addressed.

11. As people ask for a time to share faith and continue to grow in their awareness of our Catholic heritage, invite them to form a group that meets once a week, gathering for coffee and a social. As they begin with prayer, use the Scripture readings of the day from the Lectionary, reflecting on them and offering their prayers, their general intercessions. They could then discuss the life of the person whose biography begins each chapter of the *United States Catholic Catechism for Adults* (they would read the chapter before gathering). As they reflect on the person's story, the church's story, and their story, these questions could guide their discussion: Where do you think the challenges are in the person's life, and how do those challenges compare/relate to the challenges in your life? How did the person respond? Does that give you any ideas, suggestions for the responses you make in your life? What questions, feelings, and thoughts do you have after reading this chapter about our faith?

12. Gather a group of people to meet over lunch once a month, creating a space where, through discussion, they can become more aware of global realities, realities that will touch our futures, those of our children, our planet, and all people. One resource that might be used is *50 Facts that Should Change the World 2.0* by Jessica Williams.[1] This simple but powerful book is a compilation of fifty facts about the state of the world today. Sources are provided for each fact, which is followed by a short essay that fills in details. Though some of the facts are funny, most are disturbing, and all could be the basis for discussion.

13. Each year a "Conversation Week" is held throughout the world. Use or adopt these ideas in your adult formation programming by planning to take part in next year's worldwide Conversation Week. Be sure that each of your adult gatherings has time for a "Conversation Café"; plan your own Conversation Cafés around significant questions for your faith community.[2] These are a few of the many questions suggested for the past years' Conversation Weeks:

> What can we do to reduce or eliminate violence in the world?
>
> How can intangibles like values and beliefs tangibly contribute to solving the problems of our times?
>
> What will it take to achieve world peace? Not just end war, but wage peace? What would a peace army look like, and what would it do?
>
> How do we shift from "me" to "we" on both the local and global levels?
>
> What do you stand for, truly stand for?

What helps you have energy and hope in these times?

If indeed most of us want peace, why don't we have it?

14. Coordinate "Scripture Alive All Week Long." In addition to "Question of the Week," which we explored in chapter 4, another method to help stay focused on the Scripture readings is to suggest a different question for each day of the week. These questions could be based on the Scriptures just heard or on the readings for the upcoming Sunday, enabling people to begin preparing themselves to hear the Word proclaimed. Prepare a handout with the reading broken into seven segments, followed by a reflection question, bringing it into focus for today's life. As you begin this process, it might be best to have this on a "Prayer Reflection Sheet" and personally hand it to each parishioner. After people have become familiar with it, it could be in the bulletin, in a very prominent place. (These reflection sheets might provide the opportunity for some people to come together and pray with the Scriptures once a week, reflecting on what the readings mean in their lives.)

15. There are new films continually being released (in the major markets or through religious publishing companies, etc.) that provide opportunities for small faith-sharing groups. How might some of them be used in your parish?

16. It has been said that if you give workshop participants a set of handouts, the workshop is a success. What about those, then, who aren't able to participate in the parish (or diocesan) workshops, discussion groups, Scripture study, etc.? Can we still make use of the potential of handouts? They might be short: a phrase from Scripture, a line from a social justice teaching, a word of wisdom from someone from the communion of saints—on a bookmark, a bumper sticker, a billboard. They might be longer: a thought for each day of the week, a practical idea for Christian living at home and at work, background information and reflection questions on the Sunday readings—on a page inserted in the weekend bulletin and/or on your parish website, or shared with parishioners (and others) through Facebook or Twitter.

17. This practical procedure of handouts could also be expanded to include a series of handouts and other resources as well as personal support that is made available to parishioners through the myriad communications available today (mail, cable, print, audio, video, email, social media, etc.). Thus, we have distance education! Given our rural communities, homebound individuals, people with busy schedules and long commutes—all with CD players, MP3 players, iPods, apps, and tablets/laptops—we have many opportunities that are ripe with new ways for learning.

18. Many parishes organize visits to their parishioners on a regular basis. These can be done by the pastoral team, pastor, and/or parishioners on a visitation committee. When the visit takes place, can things be done to intentionally help ongoing faith development? Are parishioners asked about their interests so that materials can be sent or opportunities shared that might answer their questions or connect them to groups that can help deepen their faith? Audio/videos of various talks, reflections, and the Sunday liturgies can be taken to the shut-ins. The visitors can spend some time talking to them about the resource on their next visit.

19. Capitalize on the phenomenon of today's coffee shops and set up a coffee café that is open at appropriate times for your parish (e.g., during faith formation programs for children, the drive time after work, in between weekend liturgies, Sunday afternoons or early evenings). A facilitator can begin a topic and then invite questions, comments, and conversations from those who stop by, keeping the environment and process informal and participatory.

20. Watch for unique happenings within our everyday culture. How might we use these opportunities to connect faith to life? For instance, each year around the world on September 21 the International Day of Peace is celebrated; what might we do to help adults study, reflect on, and talk about the various circumstances today that stand in the way of peace? How might we share with adults the riches we have within Scripture and our tradition to be peacemakers?

On October 24th, a large coalition of groups encourages the celebration of Take Back Your Time Day, which challenges time poverty and overwork in America. The website, *Take Back Your Time*, offers a group of speakers.[3] Would a workshop be helpful for your adults? In what other ways (via your website, Sunday bulletin, articles, etc.) could you engage adults in reflection upon this reality of our lives and our Christian call to cherish and observe Sabbath time?

April 22nd is the observance of Earth Day, another international observance that is interrelated to our theology about God and creation. How might we use the observance to deepen adults' understanding—and actions—for care of creation?

21. The function of marketing/publicity is to attract people to the offerings. One of the ingredients of the marketing endeavor is enticing titles. This can be the first thing that grabs people's attention and convinces them to pay attention and read on. Some of these might work for your parish:

Justice: Inviting the World to the Church Social

Family Fights Don't Have to Be Fatal: Facts for Fair Fighting

What to Do if Your Spouse is Cool Toward Religion: Sparking Interest in Your Mate's Faith

Jesus was Fully Human—Are You?

Does One (Prayer) Size Fit All?

Guess Who's Coming to Dinner: Jesus' Meals and Social Justice

Finding God When Life's Not Fair

Mary-Ways for Pain-Filled Days

Prayer Is Not a "Peaceful" Means

Vocation: The Difference between House and Home

Marriage and Money: Until Debt Do Us Part

Kids Are Worth It: Parenting with Wit and Wisdom

How to Forgive Absolutely Everyone of Everything

The God I Don't Believe In

Letting Our Imaginations Soar: What Makes Us Catholic

Five Great Heroes of the Bible, Who Happen to Be Women

A "Titanic" Struggle: Film and TV and the Battle for Minds and Hearts

We Can Build a Better World, But Do We Want To?

Blessings, Balance, and a Sense of Humor: Living Somewhat Steadily in an Unsteady World

God Uses Cracked Pots

Cloak the Earth with Prayer

Whatever Happened to the Church I Knew?

Today's Stressful World Can Be Hazardous to Your Health

Look Beyond the Bread You Eat

Reflection/Conversation Starters

- Which of these events/gatherings are already happening within our parish's adult faith formation program?
- Have any of them surfaced as needs/interests as we have done needs assessment within our parish? If not, check with parishioners. Would people be interested in any of these? Why? Why not?

📖 What other ideas surface from the various interests and needs that are expressed to us, our committee, and other parish leaders?

📖 How would these ideas work in our parish? What would be the first step(s) to begin putting things in place for one (or more) of these to be a success?

📖 Are there small groups currently meeting in our parish? What do they study? How do they pray? How do they serve?

📖 Might there be small group meetings of which we are not aware?

📖 Might there be parishioners who would like to live their faith by being in a small group for prayer? for study? for service/action?

📖 Could some of our adult faith formation offerings be structured around the form of Conversation Cafés?

📖 Would one-question-a-day for Scripture readings be helpful for our parishioners? Is there someone within the parish who would like to coordinate this project?

📖 Would film-study-discussion groups be interesting for some of our parishioners? Who in our parish would be interested in searching out films and their study guides?

📖 What events/observances within our culture can be springboards for adult formation for our parishioners?

📖 What intriguing titles do we/will we use? Titles that say enough to capture people's interest and make them say, "That's exactly what I'm feeling, thinking, needing . . .""I need to learn more about that . . ." "I want to talk with others about that . . ."

Hands-On Helps

🐚 One method of adult faith formation today, of course, is the invitation of guest speakers to join with our parish communities, to share their wisdom, their experiences, to walk with us on the faith journey. The preparation and details that accompany this are crucial, not for the person invited but for the participants. Janet Schaeffler, "Hospitality in Adult Faith Formation (Part 4)," *GEMS: Great Endeavors Mined & Shared* 18 (April 2012), http://www.janetschaeffler.com/GEMS__18.pdf, provides a "checklist" that we might use.

🐦 For some further ideas regarding art and adult faith formation, see Schaeffler, "An Ecumenical Conference and Art Exhibit," *GEMS* 49 (January 2015), http://www.janetschaeffler.com/GEMS__49.pdf.

Notes

[1] Jessica Williams, *50 Facts that Should Change the World 2.0* (New York: Disinformation, 2007).

[2] *Conversation Week*, http://www.conversationweek.org/why-conversation-week; *Conversation Circles* "Conversation Café," http://conversationcircle.com/?page_id=6.

[3] *Take Back Your Time*, https://www.takebackyourtime.org.